What Ever Happened To My Prince Charming?

What Ever Happened To My Prince Charming?

How to re-identify the man you fell in love with and have the marriage you desire.

Misty Stanczyk

BELIEVERS PRESS

What Ever Happened To My Prince Charming?
 Self-published through Believers Press.

Book design by Brion Sausser

ISBN 978-0-578-04274-9
Library of Congress Control Number: 2009912711
Printed in the United States of America

Dedication

To my Grandparents, Walter and Inez Roth-

The example you set for me and all of our family
is a gift I will always cherish!
(67 years of marriage before my Grandpa passed and
went to live with our Father in Heaven)

To my Parents, Morris and Marcy Haase-

I am so thankful that God blessed me with the
parents that He did. I am so proud of you and
honored to be your daughter!!

To Alex, My Prince Charming-

Chapter 20 is specifically dedicated to you!

To Keola, Ashlei and Kai-

Each of you is a special and remarkable gift from God.
I am so incredibly thankful to be
your Mommy!!

Thank You!

This book would not have been possible without the help and support of so many people.

First, a very special thanks to my family, Alex, Keola, Ashlei and Kai. Alex supported me in my dreams and efforts and managed gallantly when I fled the country to do my research or attend conferences. Not once did he complain about the extra work it brought his way. And my babies have willingly given up time for me to complete this project. This was a whole family effort and I appreciate you so much!! And Alex, the money you invest regarding this book and my passion for orphans and Acacia Village is so generous. Thanks so much for believing in me.

To my core team of ladies who have supported me through the process: Corrina Burris, Juli Christo, Marcy Haase, Nicole Haase, Miracle Hoff, Kari Hoefer, Nelly Penalonzo and Penny Sienkiewch. Your friendship, support, and input have been so appreciated. I look forward to stepping ahead with you in a walk of faith with Grrls4God!

To Penny Sienkiewch, you were a gift from God when you took my call eight years ago. You generously gave up your time to work with Alex and me at a very dark time in our lives. There is nothing I could ever do to repay you for the part you played in healing our marriage. Your faith and passion are astounding and my prayer is that some of that will wear off onto me. You are truly a remarkable woman!

To all of the people who helped review, make recommendations and graciously share their time and prayers: Corrina Burris, Juli Christo, Karin Ehrhorn, Kristie Emerson, Louis and Sara Fawcett, Matt and Nicole Haase, Simon and Amanda Heapes, Sara Held, Kari Hoefer, David and Miracle Hoff, Michael and Dawn Hooks, Rick and Katie Hutchcroft, Jan Kalliainen, Linda Koepplin, Jeff and Tracy Marshall, Penny Monetti, Marvin and Gribdia Nelly Penalonzo, Scott and Penny Sienkiewch, Corrin Stevens, Kandi Jo Rivinius Trace, Paul E. Tsika II, Michael and Selena Stanczyk, Alexandria Walkinshaw, Jack and Stephanie Weinzierl, Cherie Weishaar, Dirk Wierenga and James and Kelly Wilson. Inevitably I have left someone's name out of this list and for that I am truly sorry. Everyone's participation really means so much to me!!

To my sister, Miracle Hoff, who did multiple edits of this book for me. Not only did you get beauty in our family, but also more than your fair share of the brains;) I am so proud of you for all you have accomplished both professionally speaking as well as raising your awesome five kids and taking great care of David. I am so proud of you and appreciate you so much. I note here, that my use of smileys and winks at the end of sentences was against the advice of my sis;)

To Dawn Hooks and Jennie Slack for schooling me on commas and helping with editing, your expertise and literary abilities are most appreciated. I dislike commas and punctuation even more now, after coming near the completion of this book. At this time I must disclaim that any errors in this book, grammatical or otherwise, are totally my responsibility. I wrote this book with the intention of writing it as I would speak it…due to that, there are certain to be errors that have been overlooked or are just who I am.

To Juli Christo for doing the final edit with me, while we tanned by the pool. Multi-tasking is what we call it;) “Ut-oh…Ut-oh… Ut-oh” I thoroughly enjoyed the experience;) I appreciate you so much!

To Brion at www.bookcreatives.com for going above and beyond to pull off my book design. Your patience and efficiency is so beyond ordinary, and your talent and vision is extraordinary!

To Paula Ashkenazi, owner of Talkin’ Heads Beauty Salon in Clayton, Panama, thanks for working so hard to keep me blond to match my personality. Your staff, specifically Luis, Lissi and Rigo, are remarkably talented and so appreciated.

To Verna Kokmeyer and the Maranatha Christian Writers’ Conference, for helping me understand the publishing world a bit more and sending me off in the right direction. Attending your conference was a great decision. Verna, your willingness to serve while overseeing such a remarkable conference still blows my mind. Leona must be smiling down on you from heaven. For any writers out there, I highly recommend the Maranatha Christian Writers’ Conference that is held in the fall of each year. For more info visit: http://www.writewithpurpose.org/ .

To Yosi and Joe in Ethiopia, thank you for hauling me around your beautiful country. I can’t wait until we return again!

A very special thank you to Louis Faucet for all of your time, insight and encouragement. Our shared belief and vision for Acacia Village is so cherished. What an honorable and awesome man you are (standing alongside your amazing and supportive wife Sara)!!

To Jamie Ford, in Muskegon, MI: The impact you have had on my life is more than I can share here. But I do believe we will be working closely together in the future. I so believe in you and appreciate you so much!!

To Brad and Julie Duncan and the World Wide Group, thank you for everything you taught us in regard to marriage, personal growth and business during the time we were with your organization. The lessons during that time have helped to shape our life today, and for that I will always be thankful.

And last, but most important, I thank God my Father- for loving me unconditionally, forgiving me for the many mistakes and bad choices made in my life and for helping me to understand Your purpose. For persistently and patiently dealing with me as I fought the idea of this book and negotiated with You regarding what I thought my purpose should be. For healing me in the areas I needed healing and for helping me to put myself out there and realize that I ultimately serve an audience of One.

Note from the Author

After completing the rough draft of this book, I made a decision to keep it short and to the point. I could take each chapter, double or triple it, and try to exacerbate the point (like we women sometimes like to do;) but in reality the answers are simple. There are simple things we can change and do that will improve the marriage and life we live today. Daily we are faced with choices. The choices we make have gotten us to where we are today. Perhaps, if you are not at a place you would like to be, it is time to make some different choices. This book isn't about being a victim or about blame. It is about choosing to move forward and striving for a blessed marriage. Most importantly it is about locating your Prince Charming who has been lost in battle. It really is a simple process if you are looking at the big picture. The problem is that too often people are unwilling to do what is hard and necessary, to get what they ultimately desire. Whether you choose to apply anything from this book is totally up to you. But keep in mind, it is all a choice. If your marriage is heading in a bad direction, and you choose not to make changes, you are not a victim. You are part of the problem. My hope and prayer is that you choose to make changes and choose to strive for all that life truly has to offer. I do believe God blesses our good choices. I do believe God wants to bless our marriages. I do believe, with God's help, you hold the key to finding and unlocking your Prince Charming from the bondage of life he is buried under.

One other comment before we get started. I am writing this book as if I am speaking with a dear friend. I am perfectly aware that there are grammatical errors. If that is something that hangs you up, you are missing the point of the book. It may also be a good sign that you might want to focus some attention on chapters 7-21. I truly mean this in a loving way: If you choose to be harsh in your judgment with the grammar in this book, I can only imagine the arrows your husband has to dodge…perhaps now is time to focus on some personal changes.

Table of Contents

PROVERBS 31:10-31

A Wife of Noble Character

10 [b] Who can find a virtuous and capable wife? She is more precious than rubies.
11 Her husband can trust her, and she will greatly enrich his life.
12 She brings him good, not harm, all the days of her life.
13 She finds wool and flax and busily spins it.
14 She is like a merchant's ship, bringing her food from afar.
15 She gets up before dawn to prepare breakfast for her household and plan the day's work for her servant girls.
16 She goes to inspect a field and buys it; with her earnings she plants a vineyard.
17 She is energetic and strong, a hard worker.
18 She makes sure her dealings are profitable; her lamp burns late into the night.
19 Her hands are busy spinning thread, her fingers twisting fiber.
20 She extends a helping hand to the poor and opens her arms to the needy.
21 She has no fear of winter for her household, for everyone has warm [c] clothes.
22 She makes her own bedspreads. She dresses in fine linen and purple gowns.
23 Her husband is well known at the city gates, where he sits with the other civic leaders.
24 She makes belted linen garments and sashes to sell to the merchants.
25 She is clothed with strength and dignity, and she laughs without fear of the future.
26 When she speaks, her words are wise, and she gives instructions with kindness.
27 She carefully watches everything in her household and suffers nothing from laziness.
28 Her children stand and bless her. Her husband praises her:
29 "There are many virtuous and capable women in the world, but you surpass them all!"
30 Charm is deceptive, and beauty does not last; but a woman who fears the LORD will be greatly praised.
31 Reward her for all she has done. Let her deeds publicly declare her praise.

Chapter 1

INTRODUCTION AND PURPOSE

Today I was thinking about how blessed I have been to be married to the man of my dreams. Reflecting on the past 15 years, remembering the good, the bad and the ugly, I ask myself how we have survived. It has been a long and bumpy road, yet today I reflect on the fact that even though there have been some extremely painful and dark times, I would go through it all over again to get to where we are today.

As I write this book, I have dear friends going through divorce or on the verge of divorce, all struggling to remember why they fell in love in the first place. I also have dear friends who are about to embark on the whole newlywed chapter. I hurt for the ones struggling and am hopeful for the ones entering their covenant marriage. With all my heart, I wish I could fix all of the problems, hurts and disappointments that they are facing now or most surely will face in the future. Well, I can't fix those, but I can offer a hopeful reality of what could be in store.

I do not claim to be an expert nor do I claim to be a counselor. I merely wish to share my experiences with the hopes that my friends will be blessed with the marriage I have experienced. I don't think it is by luck or chance that I am in a blessed marriage. I think it has been a conscious choice to love every day (or at least almost every day) and to not give up when there has been no logical reason to keep fighting forward.

To start out, I want to share that I am a Christian woman and a lot of what I have to share will come from that perspective. I do not apologize for my beliefs or experiences, but do understand that we all have different beliefs. So I offer you this: just as if you are going to the grocery store to go shopping, take what you can use and leave the rest on the shelf. If anything from this book will help just one couple experience the blessings we have been able to experience, then this has been worth my time.

I grew up on a farm in North Dakota. I was raised Lutheran and have believed in Jesus as my Savior for as long as I can remember. That is not to say I was a perfect child, nor did I grow into a perfect adult - far from it, as a matter of fact. I got married at a young age to someone I knew from high school. We were neither mature enough to be married nor did we have common goals or dreams. It was an unhealthy marriage that ended in divorce. It left scars that were carried into our future relationships, no doubt. For both parties involved.

One sad thing about divorce is that it keeps us from fixing problems that we needed to address during that relationship. The problems do not go away. You just carry them with you wherever you move on to. Whether these issues have to deal with guilt, abuse, immaturity, selfishness, vertical-alignment (or lack thereof), or whatever, they just move with you. So you walk into the next relationship already sabotaged. It is not a good place to start.

I have heard the saying that "the grass always looks greener on the other side of the fence, but you still have to mow it once you get there." Isn't that the truth....

I walked into my next relationship blindly and quite scarred from the previous. My faith was lacking, my boundaries relaxed, my self-image deteriorated, and my destination unknown. It was at this time in my life that I met my Prince Charming. He wasn't riding his white stallion or rescuing me out of my castle, but he was rescuing me nonetheless. He had dreams and visions and hope for the future, and I was intrigued. I just believed him and knew he could accomplish it all. I loved to be around him and participate in the big dreams and the bright future. I admired the man beyond anything that I could explain. I mean, don't get me wrong, I saw other writing on the wall that was not necessarily congruent with the words he was speaking, but I could see greatness in him! He was my Prince Charming!! Not everyone else could see it. I was coming through a divorce and ended up with a child from my Prince Charming. My parents were quite certain I had hooked up with the antichrist. But none of that mattered. I could see my Prince Charming. I was blinded to everything else around me. I just knew he was the one. I believed in him and just knew we would live happily ever after.

Well, let's just say that the next approximately eight years of our lives were hell. There really is no nice way to put it. Somehow my Prince Charming was eaten or stolen or something...and I quite honestly was no Princess myself. We made a lot of mistakes, had a lot of really crappy times, thought about giving up probably... several times per week. Fortunately we had both been raised not to walk away...so we both were trying to get the other to quit...with the intention that they would get the blame and we could walk away without guilt or blame.

We had some dear friends we counseled with who tried to help us through this disaster. I remember one of them telling me, "You can't fix him; you can only work on yourself." I was so tired of hearing that!! Our dear friends ended up finding a gal who counseled couples in our situation. I spoke to her several times on the phone in preparation to meet her. Every time I got on the phone with her, I tried to share how incredibly terrible my husband was and proceeded to try to explain all of the things he was doing wrong. Every time I got started, she kept turning it back on me: "Yes, but how about you?" "What do you mean, how about me? I am not the problem here! Do you have any idea what this man had done? Do you have any idea how many areas he is falling short in? Do you have any idea??" "Yes, but how about you?" I was beginning to wonder if this brilliant woman really had a clue. Then to top it all off, the day we were scheduled to meet with her for the first time, my husband and I got into another tiff and he said (I quote), "The only reason I am going to meet this woman is because I am hoping she can fix you!" It took everything in me to shut my mouth, hide my tears, and proceed with the plan to meet this woman…and it was one of the best decisions of my life. She was a Christian woman. I would describe her as a bit quirky, or perhaps unconventional is a better word, but she was passionate and steadfast and she loved the Lord. I truly believe she was a gift from God. Not once did she let either one of us elaborate on why the other one sucked. She simply took all of the issues we collectively had, and she made us take personal responsibility for each and every one. The whole experience was about working on ourselves and making ourselves better. Not about blaming and being victims. In a nutshell, that is what it came down to. We need to take responsibility for our actions, work on being a better person, and let God work on our mate. Although it didn't happen overnight, it did happen over the course of the next year or two. I won't say it was an easy road, not at all. But I will say that all of the pain and hurt we went through was all worth it to get to where we are today. I would do it all over again in a heartbeat to reach the results we have achieved. And make no mistake about this, we took personal responsibility and denied the victim to come out. Most importantly, we also had Christ involved in our marriage, which helped hold us together with a string while we were going through that process. Only by the grace and mercy of our Lord Jesus are we here today and able to share our experience. That is a fact.

So here I am, wishing to share some thoughts and experiences with the hopes that you will be able to find your Prince Charming who is somewhere within the man that you married.

Chapter 2

THE MAN OF MY DREAMS

We girls grew up dreaming about Prince Charming. We watched movies and played with Barbies and dreamt of our future…who we would marry, what our wedding would be like… we dreamed of our happily ever after. Now I know there are girls out there that this may not apply to, but for the most part, this is the case. And granted, along the way our dreams may have been hampered by events in our lives, but if we get really honest and look under our calloused layers, that dream was present. On the other hand, our "Prince Charming" was probably watching Spiderman or Ninja movies or something of a more boyish nature. They did not grow up thinking about their wedding. It is more likely that they were envisioning their warrior victories, saving a damsel (or damsels) in distress and conquering the world. We grew up with different dreams and different visions, and to expect them to mesh naturally just isn't realistic. The warrior spirit simply isn't created to focus on what our wedding dress will look like, or what flowers we will use at our wedding. The only reason they may have an opinion about the wedding cake is because they get to eat it. So to get to the point, Prince Charmings and Princesses have two totally different agendas for the most part. If we could learn to appreciate the differences rather than try to fix them, our union would probably be much less … "frictional", for lack of a better word.

When we meet and fall in love with our Prince Charming, we fall in love with the man we believe him to be. Granted, for some time, we are totally operating with blinders on. We see things we admire about our Prince Charming. He has big dreams. He wants to conquer the world. He cherishes and loves me. He is my protector. He is my hero. He is so handsome. He gives me butterflies in my stomach. I love his attention. He is charming. Often our love and admiration goes much deeper to things very specific to him. We see it when we fall in love. We believe it when we fall in love. We desire it when we fall in love. We encourage it when we fall in love. There is not a doubt in our mind that this man is something special. And he is something special. God made man to be something special. Not one man was created identical, and each man was created for a very specific purpose. We, as women, see this in our men when we fall in love. We may not even be able to put a finger on exactly what it is, but we can see it nonetheless.

And then you get married, and life happens, and you wake up and look across the bed and go, "What the heck was I thinking?" And to be fair to our guys, they go through the same thoughts. It is not because we are bad or they are bad. It is not because we made a poor decision (well, sometimes that might be the case, but that is not the topic of this book). Our Prince Charming is still under that…man. We just helped to bury him. And notice, I said "we". It is easy to lay blame and wonder if our guy was putting on a front that wasn't real, but the fact is that our interactions on a daily basis help contribute to the man he is today. His interaction helps to contribute to the women we are today. It is a joint effort. It is easy to lay blame, but blame is not going to fix your marriage or help you to see your Prince Charming again. Understanding how we contribute and being willing to work on ourselves is what will help dig that Prince Charming back out. We hold the keys that can ultimately unlock our Prince Charming and empower him to be the King he was born to be.

1 CORINTHIANS 13:4-7

4 *Love is patient and kind. Love is not jealous or boastful or proud* 5 *or rude. It does not demand its own way. It is not irritable, and it keeps no record of being wronged.*

6 *It does not rejoice about injustice but rejoices whenever the truth wins out.*

7 *Love never gives up, never loses faith, is always hopeful, and endures through every circumstance.*

1 CORINTHIANS 13:13

13 *Three things will last forever—faith, hope, and love—and the greatest of these is love.*

To give you a light bulb analogy, a light bulb has the capacity to shine brightly, but it can't do it on its own. You have to turn it on. As wives, we have our finger on that switch. We can either choose to turn it on or turn it off....

Perhaps the first question we should ask ourselves is, "Which way are we flipping the switch??"

Before we get into the different things we as wives can do, this next chapter will lay the groundwork that gives us a clue as to why we have any problems in the first place.

GENESIS 2:20-25

But still there was no helper just right for him.

21 So the Lord God caused the man to fall into a deep sleep. While the man slept, the Lord God took out one of the man's ribs[d] and closed up the opening.

22 Then the Lord God made a woman from the rib, and he brought her to the man.

23 "At last!" the man exclaimed. "This one is bone from my bone, and flesh from my flesh! She will be called 'woman,' because she was taken from 'man.'"

24 This explains why a man leaves his father and mother and is joined to his wife, and the two are united into one.

25 Now the man and his wife were both naked, but they felt no shame.

GENESIS 3:15-19

15 And I will cause hostility between you and the woman, and between your offspring and her offspring. He will strike[b] your head, and you will strike his heel."

16 Then he said to the woman, "I will sharpen the pain of your pregnancy, and in pain you will give birth. And you will desire to control your husband, but he will rule over you.[c]"

17 And to the man he said, "Since you listened to your wife and ate from the tree whose fruit I commanded you not to eat, the ground is cursed because of you. All your life you will struggle to scratch a living from it.

18 It will grow thorns and thistles for you, though you will eat of its grains.

19 By the sweat of your brow will you have food to eat until you return to the ground from which you were made. For you were made from dust, and to dust you will return."

Chapter 3

THE FALL

So, why get Biblical? Now would be a good time to review Genesis Chapters 1-3 for the full story. We get Biblical because it explains who we are today. Let's just assume, for the sake of those readers who don't necessarily buy into this theory, that the story of Adam and Eve is true. It really explains quite a bit. Follow me here:

Adam and Eve were created into a perfectly sinless world. They had it pretty good. They didn't even mind that they were walking around in the buff. Then the temptation comes, Eve eats the fruit while Adam stands by and everything changes. Now there are consequences.

It was no longer okay to be in the buff. Well, maybe the guy didn't mind but Eve was a tad bit self-conscience. But the consequences go much farther than that. The impact was physical, psychological, societal and spiritual.

The physical consequences for Eve involved childbirth. But the psychological and spiritual are really the big change. Eve and her daughters (us) now shifted their focus and desire from God to man. The translation is "your desire will be for your husband" or "your urge will be directed towards men." This isn't necessarily a reference in sexual terms but more in psychological orientation. We no longer have the direct focus on God. Now it has been shifted to that of pleasing and getting approval from men. That could be our fathers, or husbands, or even men we work with.

Now I know some women will be up in arms about this, and at one point in my life I would have argued it to the bitter end. But think about it and get honest with yourselves. Take a good hard look at your relationships with the men in your life - your father, grandfather, husband, boyfriend, boss, whatever. We spend a good portion of our lives looking for confirmation of our worth and beauty. Often this confirmation we are looking for involves some male figure. If you disagree with this "thought" with where you are today, you may have to take a look back at experiences you had when you were younger, which could have tainted your view today.

Now take it to a marriage scenario. If we get really honest with ourselves, there are two main things that women seek in a marriage or relationship. The first is security and the second is knowing that we are the most important woman in the world to our man. Granted, there are a lot of variables that can affect that picture, but if we break it down to simplest form, that is our need.

On to Adam. Just as Eve was stripped of her longing for God and that longing was replaced by man, Adam was stripped as well. Only Adam's longing was replaced by a desire to achieve and conquer by his own effort. This created the emergence of competitive desires to surpass other men, to excel, to build. Whether this is kingdoms or companies or fortune or power, men now seek to validate their worth. They seek to dominate and control, to achieve and conquer. That is a man's desire. And while women base their worth on the approval of the men in their lives, men base their worth on their accomplishments and victories.

Back to the marriage scenario. When was the last time your husband wanted to know he was loved and the most important thing in your world? Men don't operate in the same way. Men need words of affirmation and respect. They desire to be warriors and conquerors. Ultimately, they want to achieve and be the hero. When they get married, they are looking for their wife to be their biggest cheerleader, not their leader or advisor. They want to be cheered on to victory. To deny this to them is their downfall.

IN REFLECTION

- What is it that motivates your husband? (Fear of retaliation from you is not a good answer here.)
- What excites him? Is it some sort of victory or is it hearing that you love him?
- When does he seem most responsive-when you compliment some achievement or when you are complaining?
- When was the last time he had a victory?
- When was the last time you celebrated his victory?
- Do you desire for your husband to adore you and make known his love for you?
- Do you seek validation from him (or did you when you fell in love)?
- When you feel a lack of love from your husband, does it affect you? How?
- Did something happen in your past that could distort your "truthful" answers here? You had a father that didn't tell you he loved you or that he thought you were pretty? Perhaps a harsh grandfather? Previous marriage that has left you scarred?

Chapter 4

LIFE HAPPENS

Granted, when a marriage starts out, we all have the best intentions. We love and admire our husband. We believe in them and have hopes and dreams for our futures. But as time passes, the blinders slowly start coming off, and we realize some of the weaknesses of our men. It seems only natural that we try to point them out to help "better" our husband. Unfortunately, we often take the focus off of improving ourselves and start noticing Prince Charming's shortcomings. We start to correct and discuss. They call it nagging. We call it communication. After all, when our husbands aren't communicating, we don't feel very important, do we? We don't feel like we are the most important thing if they are always busy working or watching TV or playing a video game or searching the internet. We are more important than those things. Don't they see that?

This is the start of the vicious cycle. We are trying to get our husband's attention. He is not communicating very well. We get our feelings hurt. We want to talk about it. He thinks we are nagging. That is questioning his achievement and is disrespectful in his eyes. He communicates less. We get upset more. We both start looking at each other's faults. Prince Charming and Princess are no longer visible in our spouse.

Day after day, a few more walls come up around our hearts. We allow hurts and feelings of inadequacy to cause anger or bitterness.

We take our eyes off of what we could do to improve and put our eyes on what our mate is not doing (or doing wrong). Our prosperous marriage seems like it turned into a very bad dream. What in the world happened?

If our husband is feeling like a failure at home, he will try to fill that void with achievements in other areas. Often this means working more or spending time in other areas that bring achievement (even if it is just a video game or getting the attention of another damsel in distress). I don't think it is a conscious effort but merely a response to the inborn desire to achieve. If they aren't feeling success in one area, they will seek it in another. This could be video games, sports, television, pornography or affairs, just to name a few.

Meanwhile, we are questioning our own self-worth. If we are not feeling the security and adoration we desire, we try to get our fulfillment in other areas. Perhaps our focus shifts to children or work or charity. We seek out that approval in those other areas, only with a result that validates our spouse's lack of worth (in their eyes as well as our own).

The cycle keeps fueling itself until we no longer like each other or we are so hurt we won't allow ourselves to be vulnerable with each other. This road, unless we make choices to correct the problems, is headed for disaster. And unless we understand what the cause is, it is very difficult to fix. The cause isn't that we were wrong about our Prince Charming or that he was wrong about us. The cause goes back to the beginning of time, and we just need to understand what we need from each other.

IN REFLECTION

- Did things in your marriage change after the honeymoon phase?
- At what point did things start to change?
- Did you start noticing more faults in your husband?
- Did you start "nagging" him about anything?
- Do you think your effort at communicating ("nagging") helped improve your relationship or cause more problems?
- Do you believe that your good-intentioned "nagging" helped your husband feel more like a hero and a man?
- Did you notice him start to work more or play more or seek fulfillment in other areas?
- If you took all the issues you currently have with your marriage and your relationship, and you had to summarize them into one main issue, what would that be? Does it have anything to do with a lack of feeling loved and adored by your husband?

Chapter 5

TOIL WITH THE SOIL

As we discussed in Chapter 3, the fall of Adam and Eve changed our individual focuses. Let's focus right now on men, all men. Who are they? What makes them tick? What were they created for?

We know that God made man in His image. There are many amazing facets to God. We also know God made woman in His image...obviously a little different than men. By reading the Bible we can see that God is loving and kind and compassionate. He loves us, takes care of us and is nurturing, loyal and steadfast. I tend to believe those traits may have been aimed towards us women. We also see in the Bible that God is a warrior, leader, guide and creator. He is a jealous God who tells us to care for the widows and orphans. The men who are examples to us in the Bible are men who had a heart for God and went out to fight battles on one front or another. I do not recall any stories of men who were wimpy and overly-sensitive. I do not recall any stories of men who succumbed to their wife's decisions and visions. Granted, some of them could have probably used their insight, but they certainly weren't girly-men.

Look at current media, specifically movies. In general, guys just do not like chick-flicks, unless of course they might show some skin. Seriously, our guys would rather watch movies having to do with warriors or conquest or at least with some sort of shooting involved. My husband says a good movie requires "armaments per frame." I said, "What does that mean?" He said, "The number of weapons you see in each frame of the movie." I said, "Well, how many is that supposed to be?" He said, "The more the better." I would bet if you asked your husband, he could probably relate.

Consider the movies that speak to our husband -- Braveheart, The Lord of the Rings, Rudy, Remember the Titans, Facing the Giants, Gladiator, The Patriot and 300. What all of these stories have in common is overcoming incredible odds to win the good fight, defeat evil, and win the prize (aka, "the girl" in many cases).

Some of the best movies for men are ones where the prize has been taken from them. They battle seemingly insurmountable odds in a fight for their honor and remembrance (Braveheart and Gladiator were specifically this way).

But the fairy tale story is the same for men as it is for women, only men tend to see getting the girl as a by-product of the real story, which is the fight.

Men are warriors and conquerors. Men are heroes. Men want to save the damsel in distress. Men are driven by duty and honor. Men are achievers. Men want to win. Men want respect. To get women's lib and claim equality will not help your marriage. That is not to say that we are subservient or below our men; we just have different things driving our purpose. To learn to understand these things and not get defensive could do a world of wonders for your marriage and for all of your male relationships. To learn to understand and appreciate these differences could ultimately empower your husband to not only be your Prince Charming once again, but to live the life of a King in which he is respected and honored and strong and courageous, and a light for other men to look up to and strive to be like. If you had any idea the power you have in determining the future of your husband, your family and your prosperity on so many levels, I think you would be in awe. And the amazing thing is that by helping to "build" or "encourage" him, your dreams and desires tend to fall into place as a result.

If you really think about it, why would you want to hinder this desire and drive of men? Is it because of past hurts? Past men who have let you down? Past events that have formed who you are today?

What if I am right about what you just read? What if you are truly honest with yourself?? Isn't that what you ultimately really want?? Your Prince Charming?? An honorable and amazing husband who loves and adores you?? A husband and marriage and life that prospers?? A husband you respect and one who is respected by others?? In all honesty, don't you truly desire to be able to say, "Yep that is my man! Isn't he a stud? Yep, he loves me and adores me, and I know without a doubt I am the most important person in this world to him!"

Now, I must disclaim here that not all men are honorable and good. Men's values vary depending upon their beliefs. I am writing this book as a Christian woman, therefore, I assume most women reading this will be Christian women. It is not that I don't think many of these principles apply outside of our personal spiritual beliefs; it is just that we have built our marriage around Christian beliefs that we believe to be true, so not everything in here may be received willingly beyond that.

That being said, if a man is not accountable to some other moral authority, then his intentions or aspirations may not be pure. Some men are warriors and conquerors, but their priorities may be skewed and may not include their spouse or girlfriend or children. This is something you really need to know or figure out before you get into a marriage. If you have already made that leap and are finding yourself in a bad marriage, I can only direct you to what I know, and that is the Bible and Christian counselors who operate and counsel on Christian beliefs. Beyond that, I cannot make a recommendation. However, I can say that when Alex and I got together, he was not a Christian man, and the only authority he answered to was himself. Our relationship and marriage did not flourish until we both got our Christian walk figured out, and that certainly wasn't done in unison. But by the grace of God and by prayer and persistence, we did move beyond that obstacle. So, my point is, there is hope.

IN REFLECTION

- When you married your husband, would you have considered him a good-intentioned man?
- Did you notice he strived for victories, including winning you over?
- Did he appreciate the fact that you looked up to him and respected him?
- Have you noticed when he experiences failure or setbacks that it affects his interactions?
- Have you encouraged his successes and celebrated them with him?
- Have you pointed out or harped on his failures or mistakes?
- Do you really think he wants to let you down?
- Have you ever sat down and watched a warrior movie, like the ones mentioned previously, and noticed that look in his eyes that he so wanted to relate? Have you noticed how he instinctively fell into the story alongside the warrior and "good guy(s)"? I would recommend taking the opportunity to watch some movies like that with him and notice that he inherently has a warrior spirit in him, even if it is no longer outwardly evident. I would also take note of how you respond to that warrior in the movie and how much you want him to win as well. That warrior in that movie will in reality be sitting beside you....you just need to allow him to come out!

2 CORINTHIANS 6:14-16

14 Don't team up with those who are unbelievers. How can righteousness be a partner with wickedness? How can light live with darkness?

15 What harmony can there be between Christ and the devil[d]? How can a believer be a partner with an unbeliever?

16 And what union can there be between God's temple and idols? For we are the temple of the living God. As God said:
"I will live in them and walk among them. I will be their God, and they will be my people.[e]

MARK 3:25

25 Similarly, a family splintered by feuding will fall apart.

MATTHEW 13:9

9 Anyone with ears to hear should listen and understand.

Chapter 6

EQUALLY YOKED

The Bible specifically discusses marriage and partners and clearly defines where the lines should be drawn. Many of us choose to over-look these lines based on the fact that we love someone; but in doing so, we create our own mess. We pretty much raise our hand in the air and volunteer for a battle that the Bible tells us how to avoid.

I can attest to this. When we got married, our spiritual walk was neither strong nor congruent. I believed in Jesus but did not understand having a personal relationship with my personal Savior. I had experienced the "commercialized part of religion" growing up and not the personal side of having a relationship with my Lord and Savior. That being said, I did not start my marriage on the right foot. In addition, my husband and I were not of the same beliefs. Therefore, we started out our marriage without a solid foundation. Looking back, we made the choices that really led to the mess we got ourselves in. It was not so much a matter of fault as a matter of choices that led us to where we had a problem.

Taking this beyond spiritual matters, are you and your spouse in agreement in the following areas:

Children-did you want children? If so, how many?
Child rearing and discipline
Political beliefs
Hobbies

Extended family

Where to live

Finances

Vacations

Employment/business

So many times, people do not take the time or effort to truly make sure they are on common ground. Before you got married, he sure may have been cute, but that is hardly a quality that will stand the test of time and struggles. I guess the point is that if you did not address important issues before you got married, it is no wonder these issues have manifested into the thorns and disagreements you may experience today. I say all of this to help you understand why the Bible directs us to being equally yoked. It wasn't a suggestion. It was wisdom that many of us choose to overlook...and now many of us have or are paying the natural consequences.

The good news is that if you and your spouse are not equally yoked, that is not a reason to give up. It just means you are going to have to call on God all that much more. God is amazing and can take something totally broken and fix it into a beautiful masterpiece. Yes, it may take a lot of time and selflessness and an extreme amount of prayer, but with God's help, all things are possible. You got yourself into this mess and quite honestly only God can get you out...but it will take effort and work on your part. I know, from very personal experience, that there is definitely hope.

Sad to say, most people aren't willing to put in the work. In today's society, it is much easier to cut our losses and move on. But I would contend that if you aren't willing to put in the work, you will

NEVER achieve the relationship you so desire. You can argue and dispute this all you want. You can make excuses and justifications. Many of you will, and that hurts my heart, because I want you to have that relationship you desire. But honestly the choice is yours and yours alone.

IN REFLECTION

- Were you and your husband of the same spiritual beliefs when you got married?
- If not, have those differences had an effect on the conflict in your marriage?
- What do you disagree about?
- Are you seeking a relationship with Christ?
- How about your husband? Is he seeking a relationship with Christ?
- Now that the blinders are off, can you see why the Bible speaks to this issue?
- Make a list of the issues of contention in your marriage and be aware of them. Some of these issues may be valid and areas you need to address. There may also be some that are petty, which I recommend releasing and getting over.

EPHESIANS 5:33

33 So again I say, each man must love his wife as he loves himself, and the wife must respect her husband.

PROVERBS 9:13

13 The woman named Folly is brash. She is ignorant and doesn't know it.

PROVERBS 12:4

4 A worthy wife is a crown for her husband, but a disgraceful woman is like cancer in his bones.

PROVERBS 21:9

9 It's better to live alone in the corner of an attic than with a quarrelsome wife in a lovely home.

PROVERBS 21:19

19 It's better to live alone in the desert than with a quarrelsome, complaining wife.

PROVERBS 27:15

15 A quarrelsome wife is as annoying as constant dripping on a rainy day.

Chapter 7

RESPECT

If there is one topic or area to discuss that could dramatically change your marriage, it is the topic of respect. As much as we women desire love from our husbands, it is respect that they desire from us. Dr. Emerson Eggerichs wrote an extensive book called LOVE & RESPECT that addresses this subject so thoroughly. I highly recommend reading it. In simplest terms and quite honestly the simplest formula - husbands need to LOVE their wives and wives need to RESPECT their husbands. I didn't make those rules, they are biblical. And the crazy thing is if that is applied, it actually works. Imagine that. If there is one magic ingredient in locating your lost Prince Charming, that magic ingredient is giving him respect. It took me a long time to figure this out…a very long time. If you ask a man what is more important to him, either to be loved or be respected, you will find that the vast majority of men will choose respect over love. I know that sounds crazy to us as women, but it is what it is. We can either choose to embrace it or try to apply our own girly standards. Why do you think men shut down, get unmotivated, get distracted and seek other pleasures? Because somewhere along the line, they have felt disrespected. It could be disrespect from you, as well as other factors such as disrespect at work or from your children. You can love them all you want, but deprive them of respect and they will stray in one way or another. Ultimately, they will get that respect need filled one way or another.

If you have been married any length of time, you may find that respect is a hard thing to give. We tend to think, or perhaps it has been drilled into us by society, that respect is earned. That may be the case in general relationships, but when you pull out the Bible, that stipulation isn't mentioned regarding husbands. I hardly doubt that it was an oversight on God's part. There is a reason that He said what He did. Ephesians 5:33 says that husbands are to love their wife as they love themselves, and the wife must respect her husband. It doesn't say to respect your husband when he isn't being an idiot. It doesn't say respect your husband when he has earned it. It simply says respect your husband. Notice, it also doesn't say to love your husband. Of course, you should love your husband, don't misunderstand me. But I believe the reason the Bible says what it does is because respect is what your husband needs. It tells husbands to love us (their wives), which is so vital and important to us. It tells us to respect him, which is so vital and important to him.

Respect means to hold in esteem or honor; to show regard or consideration for. Now look back over your day or this last week or maybe this last month, and really think about how much respect you have shown your husband. Seriously, it is time to get honest with ourselves. Have you nagged or belittled or corrected your husband? Have you made jokes about him around friends? Have you corrected him or pointed out faults in front of your children, family or friends? Have you complained about the way he does things or his lack of doing things? Out of all the interaction you have had, how much respect have you shown your husband? Have you withheld showing him respect because you are feeling unloved or because you don't think he deserves it? You might want to reconsider your actions, because if you aren't showing your husband respect, his gas tank is probably running on empty. If he isn't getting the respect he desires at home, don't be surprised if he is magnetized to it elsewhere. Respect is vital to men.

Because the need for respect may be foreign to us, it might take a conscious effort to get into the habit. There are so many opportunities throughout the day to be able to show respect. It all comes down to your interactions with him. When he crawls out of bed in the morning, start your day out right. Perhaps have a cup of coffee ready for him. "I really appreciate how hard you work Hun, just wanted to get a cup of coffee for you before you leave for work." Tell him how much you appreciate what he does! Tell him how much you respect him and his work and how he provides for the family. If you aren't appreciative, then that is part of the problem. Honestly, you are part of the problem. Granted, things might not be ideal, but they never will be if you aren't appreciative. The Bible tells us to be appreciative and thankful. Don't just be thankful when it is something big; notice and appreciate the small things. I honestly believe one of the reasons our marriage and family have been so blessed is because we are appreciative and thankful. We notice the small stuff, little things that cost little or no money. But with an attitude of gratitude, God loves to give. Start noticing the little things your husband does or the way he interacts or anything he does. Start telling him how much you respect him…daily, if not more.

Another thing you can do is respect his likes and dislikes. If your husband doesn't like going to parties or social events, don't insist or guilt him into doing it. If he works hard all week and enjoys watching football, encourage him to watch football. "I really appreciate how much you do for our family. I know the game is on tonight, so I have some snacks ready for you and will take the kids out so you can have some focused football time." If he likes reading the newspaper in the morning, leave him alone to do it. There could be a million different ways to show respect just by letting him enjoy the things he enjoys and not giving him attitude or a guilt trip for doing it. The funny thing is, the more he feels respected, the more he will go out of his way to make sure you are feeling the love that is so important to you.

Try edifying your husband in front of family and friends. I have seen so many women make jokes in front of others at the expense of their husband. I cringe every time I see that happen. If there is one person you should make sure to uplift and edify, for goodness sakes it should be your husband. And if you slip up, immediately apologize to him. "Babe, I am so sorry. I was trying to be funny but I just realized I totally disrespected you. I am so sorry for what I said!"

One other suggestion, teach your kids to be respectful of their father. They learn their actions from us for the most part. If we are being disrespectful, they will too. If one of our kids does something disrespectful to my husband, I am immediately all over that! And my husband does the same for me. Your interactions and respect for your husband wear off on your kids, whether you are aware of it or not. By addressing this issue, not only will you help your kids in the long run, you will also show your husband that he is the highest priority, which will also show him respect.

Remember, the Bible tells us to respect our husbands. It wasn't a suggestion. There were no strings attached to the statement. I would recommend taking this to heart. Just take a look at Proverbs and see how many times there is reference to a contentious or angry or clamorous wife. Ick!! I don't want to be one of those...how about you??

IN REFLECTION

- What does respect mean to you?
- Do you think respect is important to your husband or to any man in general?
- Do you feel that respect should be earned? If so, why? Do you have the same view in regard to love; should it be earned?
- Do you think you are showing your husband respect when you are confrontational with him?
- Can you identify areas where you have shown disrespect to your husband?
- Are there areas regarding respect that you think you need to fix or improve on? If so, make a list.
- If you are unclear about where you need "respect improvement," ask your husband these questions: "Do you feel that I respect you?" "In what ways do I disrespect you?" "What can I do to show you more respect?"

PROVERBS 12:18

18 Some people make cutting remarks, but the words of the wise bring healing.

PROVERBS 16:24

24 Kind words are like honey—sweet to the soul and healthy for the body.

PROVERBS 18:21

21 The tongue can bring death or life; those who love to talk will reap the consequences.

PROVERBS 15:1

1 A gentle answer deflects anger, but harsh words make tempers flare.

Chapter 8

WORDS OF AFFIRMATION

Men need words of affirmation. It is a form of validation for them. Hmmm, I can tell you from personal experience, this was the hardest action for me to learn and apply...for several reasons.

One thing about my husband is that, since I met him, he has always been reading and growing. He has been a great example of personal growth. On the other hand, at the time we met, I probably hadn't picked up a book since college...and it is quite likely I never actually finished a book while I was there. I was not a reader, and the thought of personal development quite honestly didn't even cross my mind. At some point in our early marriage we were introduced to the book called The Five Love Languages by Gary Chapman. In this book he breaks down peoples' love languages, the way they receive love, into five categories:

1. *Words of affirmation*
2. *Quality time*
3. *Acts of service*
4. *Gifts*
5. *Physical touch*

Out of those five love languages, the two that speak most to me are acts of service and gifts. I personally feel most loved when someone is thoughtful and goes out of their way to show me that love. It could be by getting me a cup of coffee, making me a card, remembering my birthday with a card or gift, etc. I don't want to sound greedy here;) It doesn't have to cost anything other than thoughtfulness.

My husband's love languages, on the other hand, are words of affirmation and physical touch. He likes to hear positive words, some sort of verbal validation. He likes when I sit by him and rub his back or hold his hand.

With that being said, we have TOTALLY DIFFERENT love languages. I could care less if I get the verbal validation. In fact, I have a hard time accepting compliments, so I am happy to do without the verbal validation. I am not touchy feely, so it is foreign to me to naturally show my love that way (except for with my children, for some reason). See where I am going with this?? My husband could care less if I ever bought him a gift. I buy him gifts all the time, because that is how I feel loved by receiving something thoughtful. So does it surprise you that when I give him a gift and he just kind of shrugs it off, it hurts my feelings? He is not a gifts person, I am. He is a words-of-affirmation kind of guy, I am not. The point is, we have different love languages. No kidding, huh?

One thing that changed our marriage was realizing each other's love languages and learning how to fill them. I believe that made a huge difference. It really was a little thing, but it was a choice that turned our marriage in the positive direction. We could have chosen to continue showing love the way we wanted to receive it, but we chose to focus on our spouse and what they needed. Have you ever thought about this or do you have any idea what your spouse's love languages are?? If the answer is 'no' to either, I recommend getting the book and doing some "personal development" which will help your marriage. It is a choice.

In the beginning of this chapter, I mentioned I had a hard time with this whole "words of affirmation" thing for several reasons. The first was that it is not one of my love languages, so it does not come naturally to me. The second reason, and by far the hardest, was that "I didn't think he deserved any words of affirmation. He was being an idiot. He wasn't loving me the way I needed to be loved. He was making stupid decisions. He was unworthy of those words…"

If those same thoughts ever go through your mind, it is time for YOU to change. Yep, you heard me correctly…I had to change as well…one of the hardest changes of my life.

Here is the thing, all over the Bible there is reference to the words we speak over ourselves and over others. These words are words of life or words of death. I honestly believe the secret to marriage, prosperity and success comes down to this: What are you speaking?? What are you speaking over yourself? Your spouse? Your children? Your home?? Your family and friends? Your finances? Your future? Here are some examples: "He is always working and never spends time with the family." "He never helps around the house." "I look huge! What a fatty!" "I can never get this baby fat off." "The kids never listen." "All I ever do is work." "I can never count on him." "We never have any money." "I will never be able to afford my dream house." "I will have to work until I die." "My boss is a jerk." "I never get a fair shot." "This house is always a mess." "He will never get this fixed." If you make a conscious effort to notice what words come out of your mouth, I think you might be surprised. It shouldn't be a surprise if the words and statements you speak are your reality because you helped to create it.

Now, even if your husband's love language isn't words of affirmation, I still believe that your praise and appreciation and the words you speak to him and of him are vitally important to him. They are also vitally important to you, because by speaking positively to and about someone, it has an effect on how you feel about them. Although it may not be immediate, your personal thoughts will begin to reflect whatever is coming out of your mouth. If you have been speaking garbage, it is no surprise that you aren't feeling so wonderful about your man. Try speaking awesome and uplifting things, and your personal feeling will certainly follow.

When I started speaking life into Alex, our relationship changed. When I started speaking life into Alex, I changed. When I started speaking life into Alex, our circumstances changed - spiritually, emotionally, physically and financially. It wasn't all overnight, by any means. But I noticed changes very quickly. I noticed changes in the way he felt. I noticed changes in the way I felt, because he was more receptive to me and I in turn felt more love.

At one point in our marriage, my words were harsh. I was disappointed and didn't feel loved. Therefore I retaliated with criticism. I made my disappointments known. He was fully aware of where/how he fell short, because I pointed it out to him.

Please understand, my whole desire during the time that I spoke such harsh words was just to feel loved by Alex. That is really all I wanted. I wanted to know I was loved and that I was the most important woman in the world to him. That is all I truly desired. But my method of trying to get that was way off. I believe somewhere in the male/female disconnect, this is where a lot of us get hung up.

So, my next question to you is...if I told you that you could have an incredible marriage by speaking life into your husband and making the first move, would you be willing to stop the nagging/correcting/leading/directing? Would you be willing to put your heart on the line and make the first change that could inevitably change your marriage and your life? I truly believe by speaking life into your husband and getting rid of the habit of criticizing and nagging, it will change your world. Aren't you tired of seeing the less-than-perfect version of your husband?? Aren't you tired of seeing the beaten down, worn out, disconnected, emotionally retardant side of your husband?? I honestly believe you hold the key to a successful marriage and a brilliantly successful Prince Charming.

IN REFLECTION

- What are you speaking to your husband?
- What are your thoughts about your husband when he is not around?
- What are your thoughts when you are disappointed or angry with him?
- Are you speaking and thinking things that you desire or negative words based on your emotions and disappointment?
- Do you believe that what you think and speak will come to fruition?
- Can you see how your spoken words or thoughts about your husband manifested in the man he is today?
- If it is true that the words you speak and thoughts you think manifest into your reality, do you think the path you are on will bring good results in your future?
- Make a list of recent thoughts and words and reflect on what you are truly saying and thinking. Perhaps keeping a piece of paper out to record your conversations and thoughts for a few days might be a good idea. I think you will be surprised how naturally the negative spills out of us until we make a conscious effort to grow and change it.

Chapter 9

SUBMISSION
(THAT AWFUL WORD)

Okay, I mentioned I had a hard time with the whole "words of affirmation thing". Let's just dive right into another topic that women struggle with: SUBMISSION. That is like a four letter word to so many women. It has been distorted and violated in so many ways.

Let's just say up front, submission does NOT mean doormat. There was a time that I would have argued this to the death. Submission, in the way that I am referring to, means yielding authority and showing respect.

Now let's look at what the Bible says about submission:

1 CORINTHIANS 11:3

3 But there is one thing I want you to know: The head of every man is Christ, the head of woman is man, and the head of Christ is God.[a]

1 CORINTHIANS 11:8-9

8 For the first man didn't come from woman, but the first woman came from man. 9 And man was not made for woman, but woman was made for man.

EPHESIANS 5: 22-24

22 For wives, this means submit to your husbands as to the Lord. 23 For a
husband is the head of his wife as Christ is the head of the church. He
is the Savior of his body, the church. 24 As the church submits to Christ,
so you wives should submit to your husbands in everything.

1 TIMOTHY 2:11-15

11 Women should learn quietly and submissively. 12 I do not let women teach
men or have authority over them.[b] Let them listen quietly. 13 For God
made Adam first, and afterward he made Eve. 14 And it was not Adam
who was deceived by Satan. The woman was deceived, and sin was the
result. 15 But women will be saved through childbearing,[c] assuming
they continue to live in faith, love, holiness, and modesty.

1 PETER 3:1-2

1 In the same way, you wives must accept the authority of your husbands.
Then, even if some refuse to obey the Good News, your godly lives will
speak to them without any words. They will be won over 2 by observing
your pure and reverent lives.

COLOSSIANS 3:18-19

18 Wives, submit to your husbands, as is fitting for those who belong to the
Lord. 19 Husbands, love your wives and never treat them harshly.

Okay, I can already hear the groaning. Especially reading from Timothy, that may be a bit confrontational;) But here is the thing, you have to look at the whole picture. Scripture lays things out in small pieces, and those pieces together make a whole. You can't just pull one verse and consider that foundation. You take all the verses you can find and apply that to the big picture. The big picture is quite amazing if you are willing to take a look. The problem is that some women get hung up on one passage and because of that, they never reach their full potential. That applies to marriage, family, everything. That applies to life. Some women will reach Timothy and throw in the towel. That is a choice…but one I would suggest lacks wisdom and discernment. Do you really want to have an incredible marriage or are you willing to accept defeat because you got hung up on a bible verse?? Again, the choice is yours….

Now, if you haven't flung this book across the room, if you look closely above, the word submission does not just apply to women. It clearly applies to men as well. There are all sorts of philosophical arguments we could get into over the word. But what if I told you that "submission" is one of the most powerful tools/gifts a woman could give her husband? No, I am not crazy. If a woman can let down her guard and learn to submit to her husband, in a healthy way, that submission can empower her husband to heights of confidence that will lead him to succeed in all areas of his life. By submitting to my husband, I show him respect. By feeling respected and knowing I am backing him up, my husband has excelled in every area of his life. He, in turn, has also loved and cherished me, which is priceless and worth every "sacrifice" I have had to make in regard to submission.

I believe submission and respect go hand-in-hand. If you are unwilling to submit to your husband, how can you possibly show him respect? If respect is the one thing that he needs (the same way we need to feel loved) and you are unwilling to submit, I would contend that you have a huge part of the blame if your marriage is not where you would like it to be. So, again I raise the question, do you really want an incredible marriage and desire to feel loved by your husband?? If the answer is yes, you need to get over whatever hang-ups you have with submission. It is as simple as that.

In our relationship, submission has been accomplished over time. It wasn't an instant and immediate choice for me. I had my way of doing things and if Alex didn't agree, then it was just too bad. No wonder we went through years of conflict. By my lack of submission, I showed him disrespect and lack of trust. Most importantly, rather than empowering him to be the incredible man and warrior he is, I sent him an entirely different message.

I am ashamed to say that I challenged him for control, and without even realizing it, I sabotaged his success and achievement by my selfishness. As a consequence of that, I was also sabotaging myself and had no one to blame but me. I can tell you now, even if we don't agree on something, I always willingly yield final authority and decision-making to him. I express my opinions and feelings on the matter at hand, and he listens to what I have to say. Beyond that, I yield to him and accept the outcome, whether good or bad. The funny thing is (which I doubt is a coincidence), is that my willingness to yield has the majority of the time yielded the best possible outcome. He knows if the outcome isn't positive, I won't say a word to him about it or rub it in and say, "I told you so." He doesn't make the decisions based out of fear of my retaliation. He learns if the outcome is bad and we celebrate if the outcome is good. That one little choice, to yield and submit, has had a significant impact on our marriage and our prosperity in other areas as well.

I don't care if you are the bread-winner in the family, if you have a stronger personality, if your mom didn't submit to your dad, or even if there wasn't a father figure in your family. There can only be one leader of your family, and if that isn't your husband, then I believe you are making a choice that lacks wisdom. Of course, there will be some situations that this doesn't apply to, but generally speaking I believe it to be true. I have yet to hear a woman tell me, "I so respect and admire my weeny girly-man of a husband." A man cannot bow down to the authority of his wife and still have confidence, strength and self-respect. So, if you are unwilling to submit, you are digging your own grave. Is that what you really want??

We, as women, need to get over ourselves and our own hang-ups, and allow our men to be men!

IN REFLECTION

- Do you have a problem with the word submission? Why is that? Who in the past has hurt you in a way that submission seems to be a bad thing?
- Are there issues from your past that have tainted the thought of submission? Have you sought help and healing to deal with this pain or hurt?
- What does submission mean to you?
- Have you ever submitted to your husband? If so, and you no longer do, what caused that to change?
- Would you be willing to make a conscious effort to submit or yield to your husband? If it could improve your marriage, would you be willing to change your ways?
- If submitting to your husband empowered and uplifted him, why would you withhold this gift from him?
- In what ways could you make changes now? What are some areas that you fight for control? You don't have to do everything at once, but perhaps take one example and willingly submit (not just for a day but for an extended period of time). Note any changes you see in your relationship in regard to that.

Chapter 10

VULNERABILITY

Okay, let's take another look at Prince Charming. Prince Charming is a hero; he saves his damsel in distress. In order for her to be saved, she is in some vulnerable situation. Think back to the stories of Cinderella, Sleeping Beauty, and Beauty and the Beast. They tend to be some of the most popular fairy tales or folktales that trace back hundreds of years.

Cinderella lost her mother at an early age. Her father then remarried. Depending on which version of the story you read or movie you saw, her father may have been present or something might have happened to him. What is consistent throughout the story, Cinderella's stepmother was not a kind woman. And her stepsisters were not nice either. Cinderella went from being loved and well cared for to serving and taking care of her stepmother and stepsisters. There was a ball to be attended by all of the fair ladies of the land. Cinderella didn't even consider attending because she had nothing to wear and her self-image wasn't so good. The fairy godmother arrives on the scene and before you know it, she is all decked out with a beautiful dress and the accessories to boot. She attends the ball knowing life would return to normal at the stroke of midnight. The Prince was enthralled with her from first sight. At the stroke of midnight, she flees accidently leaving one of her glass slippers behind. The Prince finds it and searches the land to find his love. When Cinderella tries on the glass slipper, it fits. She is turned back into the beautiful princess on the outside and reflects the beauty she always had on the inside. She and her Prince Charming get married...and live Happily Ever After.

Sleeping Beauty is the story of a beautiful little princess who was the joy of her parents. She was gifted with many things such as beauty and wit and charm. She was loved by all, except the evil fairy who put a spell on her. Again, there are different versions to this story, but what inevitably happened is that when she was reaching adulthood she pricked her finger on a spindle and fell into a deep sleep. Briars sprang up around the castle and no one could enter it for one-hundred years. At the end of the one-hundred years, a prince who had heard of her story of enchantment went to the castle in search of her. Upon seeing her and her beauty, he fell to his knees and kissed her. She awoke to his kiss, they fell madly in love ...and they lived Happily Ever After.

In Beauty and the Beast, a merchant went out to conduct his business. Before leaving his daughters, he asked each what they desired for him to bring on his return. The youngest daughter was Belle, named because she was so lovely and pure of heart. She was her father's little Princess. Her desire was for her father to bring her a rose. He set off to attend his work, and on his return he is lost and must seek shelter. He finds shelter in a large castle where he was provided for with hospitality. When he was ready to depart he noticed a beautiful rosebush outside the castle and went to pick a rose for his little Belle. Upon taking a rose, he was confronted by the Beast. What we don't see at this time is that the Beast was once a happy little boy, until he lost his father and mother. He was cursed and became the Beast. Again, depending which story you have read or seen, the merchant's punishment inevitably leads to Belle living in the castle with this Beast. She accepts her life as it comes. Although at first she was quite frightened by the Beast, she eventually grows to love him in a friendly sort of way. After getting homesick, the Beast allows her to go visit her family under the condition that she return to him. When she doesn't return as promised, the Beast almost dies. When she finally gets to him, she is so distraught by the thought of losing him. She tells him she loves him and magically before her eyes, she sees him transform into a handsome prince…and they live Happily Ever After.

What did they all have in common? They were vulnerable and they needed saving. And notice in some stories, it took the Princess to bring the true Prince Charming to light. The Prince or hero in all of those stories was there to save their Princess and ultimately love her. Every one of the Princesses was vulnerable. They all needed to be rescued in some way. They were submissive. They didn't have input on how they needed to be rescued…they didn't critique the rescue… they didn't provide a more efficient solution - they just needed.

We as women, whether we admit it or not, desire to be rescued, wanted and loved. But often times, life leaves us calloused. These calluses put up walls that hide hurts and disappointments. We tend to self-preserve at some point by no longer showing our vulnerability to our husbands. Unfortunately, this is a double edged sword. We desire rescuing and love, but we are afraid of being hurt so we hide that. Our husbands at some point (depending on how not observant they are being) realize that we are no longer vulnerable to them. Since they, by nature, want to be the heroes, rescuers, conquerors, whatever you want to call it, they no longer see a need to be filled. Our lack of vulnerability leads to a lack of respect and lack of willingness to submit. From their point of view, their damsel in distress is no longer vulnerable. In their view, she may be naggy, complaining and strong. The bottom line is they no longer see a need to be filled. And as much as we would love for them to get a clue and realize that the only reason we are acting in the way we are is because we need them to show us the love we so strongly desire, chances of them catching that clue are not very likely. We must help them along.

Not to slam on guys at all, but sometimes they really just don't get us. It is not their fault; that is just the way God made their brains. Our discreet or not so discreet hinting at our need for their love is wrongly transposed as us showing them disrespect, not being submissive or vulnerable, and not needing them. Since they generally don't compute this through our nagging (communication), their take on the whole situation is totally different than what we want them to be getting.

So, what is the solution? I say the solution is sucking it up and working on ourselves. Working on our willingness to show them our vulnerability. Working on trying to see things from their perspective and not jumping to our own girl conclusions of what their actions mean. I do believe husbands want to love their wives. I do believe they want to rescue and save their wives. I do believe they want to be the Prince Charming we desire. I just think that they are tired of failing once again in our eyes, so they despair and see their attempts as futile.

If we are having struggles in this area, how do we fix this?? To start out with, turn to God, because He is always the first solution. Ask God to take the calloused layers of your heart away and show you how you can be vulnerable once again. Ask God to work on your husband and give him the opportunity to do some rescuing again. Stop nagging or correcting or offering efficient solutions to how he should be rescuing. If your sink needs repair and he is trying to fix it, let him. Let him figure out for himself that he needs to call the plumber. Don't offer that insight. Stop having expectations of how and when you think something needs to be done. And when he does something, I don't care how small it is, praise him! Praise him and thank him for taking care of you. Let him know how much you appreciate his valiant efforts, even if they are little, because if your reception is right, his small effort of rescue will lead to bigger ones. In the process, not only will you give him purpose and confidence back, but he can and probably will excel from there.

Remember, what is the goal of reading this book? To get your Prince Charming back! To uplift and encourage him to the greatness that God created him for. To receive the love and security and intimacy you desire. Right? So there is nothing wrong with being a little vulnerable if it achieves our desired results.

IN REFLECTION

- Do you show vulnerability to your husband?
- Do you express to your husband that you need him?
- Is there something from your past that has deterred you from showing vulnerability? If so, who or what?
- Have you ever told your husband something along the lines of, "Honey, you are my hero and I don't know what I would do without you." "Thanks so much for helping me taking the garbage out. It was so heavy I couldn't lift it. I really appreciate your strength and your help." Sometimes you just need to get creative. Take any simple example of your need and thank him for filling it.
- Do you seek out your husband's advice or direction in anything?
- What areas or examples can you think of that you could show your vulnerability and allow him to come to the rescue?

Chapter 11

STOCK IN HEADACHE MEDICINE

"Honey, I've got a headache", or whatever your excuse is, has got to stop!! Remember, you want a better marriage, right? If you want a better marriage, you need to hook your husband up. Men, by nature, are visually stimulated and sex to them is a form of respect and validation. That is a fact, and anyone who argues with it is lying to themselves. We, as women, on the other hand, seek out intimacy and emotional connection with our man. To put it in the simplest terms possible, men's "leetle" brains do not comprehend this. If you want intimacy and emotional connection with your husband, you can't hold out in the sex department. Sorry, but if you are not satisfying your man, someone or something else will.

I know life is busy. We have business, jobs, children, responsibilities, blah, blah, blah. I know. I really do. We have three children and are in the process to adopt more. We have several businesses that we operate. There are always appointments, driving the kids around, shopping, cleaning, running errands…the list can be extensive. I truly get that. But in a marriage, your highest priority, next to God, should be your husband. I didn't make the rules. God did. And if you want to achieve the fulfilling marriage you desire, you might need to make some changes.

I see it time and time again. Once we have children, our focus changes from our husbands to them. Don't get me wrong, they should definitely be a priority, but elevating them above your husband will not contribute to a successful marriage.

Often times, if we are feeling a lack of love from our husband, the first thing we do is close the sex department. Emotionally, that seems like the right thing to do. I can understand where you are all coming from. But that will not fix any problems; it will only add to them.

PROVERBS 5:19

19 She is a loving deer, a graceful doe. Let her breasts satisfy you always May you always be captivated by her love.

1 CORINTHIANS 7:3-5

3 The husband should fulfill his wife's sexual needs, and the wife should fulfill her husband's needs. 4 The wife gives authority over her body to her husband, and the husband gives authority over his body to his wife. 5 Do not deprive each other of sexual relations, unless you both agree to refrain from sexual intimacy for a limited time so you can give yourselves more completely to prayer. Afterward, you should come together again so that Satan won't be able to tempt you because of your lack of self-control.

Here is another example of a choice we make that contributes to where we are in our marriage. Sometimes…often times, if you want to have control of where your marriage is headed, you will need to "take the high road" or make sacrifices or choose to do things that you don't necessarily want to do. Why? Because you love your husband, and you want an incredible marriage.

Looking at things from a man's perspective which is TOTALLY different than our own, sex is important to him. Sex is a sign of respect. Sex gives a man confidence. Sex validates his manhood. Sex keeps his attention at home where it should be rather than seeking fulfillment elsewhere. With that being said, why would you want to show him disrespect...affect his confidence negatively...invalidate his manhood...encourage him to seek sexual fulfillment elsewhere?? Need I say any more on that?

I understand there are situations where marriages are unhealthy - women are dealing with past sexual issues or there are medical issues involved as a reason for not having sex. This book is not addressing those issues. If that is something you are dealing with, you will need to seek answers elsewhere. But for those of us who are just emotionally depleted or simply upset with our husbands, sex should not be used as a tool to try to get him to behave the way you want him to. It will never work in the long run, and you are making a choice that could contribute significantly to a failed marriage.

Taking a closer look at sex and contributing to a man's confidence, I truly believe this is one area that can have a significant impact on our husbands. If a man, by nature, seeks to save a damsel in distress and conquer the world (or whatever it is they are trying to conquer), doesn't it make sense that a man who is getting some from his Princess is more empowered to go out and take on the world? Let's look at it from the other perspective. If a man would like to have sex with his wife and she turns him down, has he just conquered or been conquered? How can we possibly expect our husbands to go out and successfully conquer life, their businesses, their jobs, etc, if they can't even conquer the one woman who means the most to them? How are they supposed to feel leaving the house for a big meeting knowing they just got disrespected and trampled on or turned down by their wife? Yet we want them to go out, be successful, make money, buy us flowers, be romantic, get promoted, take us on nice vacations, buy us jewelry (hint hint baby, haha!), etc. We want all the good things that come from a successful man, but we kick him out the door sexually frustrated and wonder why he loses his lack of drive? You might want to think about your contribution to the confidence and strength of your husband the next time you are ticked off with him for not being more emotionally in-tune with you…

A very common trait of men is that they are visual. We, being more emotional, do not put as much stock in what we are…looking at. That being said, I believe sex and visual stimulation from us as wives is important. When you were dating, I am guessing, you probably fixed yourself up before going on a date with your husband. You fixed your hair, put nice clothes on, brushed your teeth…you made an effort to look attractive for your man. Then you got married. Still put effort (sometimes) in putting yourself together. Then what happened? Sweats became more comfortable, hair got brushed out if you had to leave the house. What happened? Inevitably at some point in our relationship, we get comfortable or lazy, and we do not put the same effort into looking attractive for our husbands. I understand and can totally relate to this. It happened to me too. The point is that just because we get comfortable or lazy, doesn't make it okay to stop taking care of ourselves. Often times we put effort into looking nice to leave the house for our jobs or for church or whatever. But what about our husbands? Shouldn't they be the most important thing? Shouldn't we make the effort to look nice for them? It is time to make them a priority again. We can come up with all kinds of excuses for why we do it. Excuses are nothing but excusing ourselves for being less than we can be. We want our husbands to love us and communicate with us and provide us with our emotional fulfillment, but then we make excuses for looking like crap when we are around them. If you want a great marriage, here is another area you can make a conscious choice to excel in. You would be surprised at the response from your husband if he noticed you were taking time to look nice and take care of yourself for him. How about honoring your husband by going out of your way to be visually stimulating to him? Instead of trying to impress your boss or people you are friends with, how about taking the time to impress your husband?? I can't express enough what such a small thing can do for your husband. You are showing him respect and honoring him by presenting yourself in a pleasing manner. You are giving him confidence knowing his wife goes out of her way to take care of herself. Let's face it - for the most part, his friends' wives don't do that. His competitors' wives don't do that. I would contend that it gives a husband confidence if his wife, his damsel, takes extra effort to look appealing to him. I would also suggest that it could keep his eyes from noticing other women who are taking care of themselves. Whether you like it or not, by not making the effort of presenting yourself in a manner pleasing to your husband, you are contributing to the sabotage of your relationship. Although many women don't like hearing it, the sad reality is that in this world, men are bombarded with images that are meant to catch their eye. I would encourage you to make the effort to catch his eye back to where it is supposed to be. You are contributing to his success on so many levels, not to mention helping him on a spiritual level as well.

Let's take that one step further, to the bedroom. If men are visual, it would make sense to figure out what they find sexually appealing. Every man has his own idea of what is appealing to him. I would encourage you to figure out what that is to your husband. If he is visual and likes the lights on, let there be light. If he is stimulated by lingerie or a thong or some heels, get yourself some. If you have self- image issues in those areas, get over them. It is not his fault you have those issues, so do what you can to get rid of them. If you are feeling a bit frumpy in the light, dim the light, hit the treadmill and do what it takes to get your self-image intact. It may suck to have to do, but when your sex life flourishes, you will thank me;) God created sex to be a beautiful experience between husband and wife. Get over your issues of modesty or guilt. If God created sex to be beautiful between a husband and wife, I would contend that as long as your experience is between the two of you, it will be blessed.

Another comment. Since women tend to like to warm up to sex rather than dive right in, give your husband a little grace in this area. He is clueless sometimes. But if you start to fill his needs, you will notice that your communication will get better as your relationship grows. You will be able to talk about how he could be more romantic (or whatever you are looking for). It is not that he wants to be a caveman…that is just what he knows. With time, you will be able to communicate and your sex life will improve. And if you are at the point that the thought of sex just doesn't interest you, I would highly recommend hooking your husband up anyway and saying a silent prayer to God that he would bless your union to make it enjoyable and fulfilling for you both. I do believe, if you are willing, God will bless your sex life beyond what you can imagine. But you have to be willing to put it out there for Him to bless.

In case you are wondering, before this book ever went to be published, it was reviewed by many married men. There was not one man who read this book that disputed this chapter, or any other for that matter. In fact, regarding this topic, I think most of the men who read it were relieved that it was finally addressed.

One last comment - you would be surprised the lengths your husband will go to fulfill your hopes and desires in life, if you are willing to submit yourself to him in the bedroom.

IN REFLECTION

- Do you have an active sex life? Would you and your husband answer this question the same? I would highly recommend asking him. If you don't have the same answer, this is an area to work on.
- What excuses are you using to avoid sex? By identifying these excuses, you can target the areas you need to work on.
- Do you have guilt or modesty issues based on religious beliefs? I suggest reading Song of Solomon. It might surprise you the lack of modesty and guilt in this book.
- What does your husband find stimulating? Do you know? Many women assume one thing, when in reality their husband has a totally different idea. Ask him!!
- Do you make a conscious effort to make sure your husband is getting his needs met? Are you even aware? I suggest paying attention in this area.
- What could you do differently in this area??

Chapter 12

VERTICAL ALIGNMENT

Vertical alignment was an area that was unaligned for a long time in the beginning of our relationship and marriage. It refers to our priorities and how we tackle life. According to scripture, vertical alignment should place God at the head of our homes. Following that should be our spouse, then our children. After that follows church, businesses, jobs, extended family and whatever else your priorities are, not necessarily in that order.

Too often entering a marriage, if our unions aren't entered into as a covenant under God, our marriages automatically start off on the wrong foot. We may get the spouse thing right, at least in the beginning. Then children often come along and many times they become our highest priority.

Entering the covenant of marriage under Godly principles is so important. There is a reason that the Bible talks about being equally yoked, which is discussed in another chapter. When two people enter a union and they don't agree on Biblical principals about marriage and relationships, there is no foundation for the grace and healing that is so necessary once people live under the same roof. It leads to problems that could eventually lead to divorce.

The only perfect thing going into a marriage is God. We, as sinners and humans, are far from perfect. Our spouse may have seemed perfect while we were courting, but one day you wake up and wonder who the heck you married. "What is up with the socks on the floor?" "What do you mean you can't find your underwear? Did you even look in your underwear drawer?" "Do you seriously need to pee on the seat...wouldn't it make more sense to lift the lid?" "I just fell into the toilet again - you forgot to put the lid down!" "Did you squeeze the toothpaste like that?" "I don't want to watch ESPN right now!" "No, I am not in the mood." "If you don't like the dirty dishes in the sink, why don't you wash them? Or better yet, get me a maid." "Why don't you ever want to talk? Honey, we need to have a talk." "Why don't you bring me flowers anymore?" "Do you happen to remember what today is?" "No, I am still not in the mood!!"

We are far from perfect. We have learned that about our spouse and hopefully we have figured that out about ourselves. Grace is so necessary in a good marriage.

Our spouse, next to God, should always be our priority. Always means always. It doesn't matter if you have kids involved, in-laws, jobs, whatever. Our spouse should always be in the top position under God. One of the biggest mistakes married couples make is getting our priority alignment messed up. Making our spouse a priority means taking time to be with them and not using the children/house/work/etc. as an excuse.

Many mothers will argue to the death of their marriage that their kids need to be priority. They can provide excuses and reasoning as to why this is. I would say to anyone who offers excuses, they are wrong. Our spouse is our other half. Biblically speaking, when we get married, we are joined into one. You cannot be whole and completely set apart any longer. If you are neglecting your husband to take care of your children, you are neglecting yourself and sabotaging your future. Children are incredibly important and are gifts and blessings from God. But one day they will grow up and leave your home, and you will be left with your spouse whom you have neglected for all of these years. It is no wonder many couples end up divorced after the children leave the home. They no longer know each other or share anything in common. They don't know how to communicate and probably lost that loving feeling many years prior.

Don't misunderstand me, I love and adore our babies!! But in my opinion, the best gift I can give them is a loving and respectful example of our marriage. I hope and pray our daughter marries a man like her daddy. And I can honestly say I hope our sons marry a woman like me. Not because I think I am great, but because I treat my husband with respect and admiration, and because I want our boys to get that respect, empowerment, uplifting and adoration from their wives.

Elevating someone or something to a priority over your husband is probably one of the biggest signs of disrespect you could show him. You claim to want a great marriage, you want the Prince Charming, you want to see him succeed, you want prosperity in your home…but you just chose the opposite when you chose to lower your husband on the priority list. It amazes me how many women will complain about their marriage and their spouse, not even considering the possibility that they have played a big part in getting to those complaints.

Disappointment in our spouses is unavoidable. There will inevitably be hurts and heartbreaks along the way. That is why God needs to be the priority, the head of the household. God is the ultimate example of grace. How is it that we are thankful to accept the grace God grants us, yet we are so unwilling to extend it to our spouse? Forgiveness is also another ultimate example that God shows us. He allowed His only son, Jesus Christ, to die on the cross to prove that to us. How can we expect God's forgiveness if we are not willing to extend forgiveness to our husbands? God knows, our husbands need it…but so do we;) Healing is the other thing we get from God. Only God can heal our hurts. Only God can cleanse our heart so that we can get over disappointments and hurts from our husbands. That is why God is the most important component of our relationships. Relationships outside of God will never experience the full blessings that are available to us in our marriages. And without setting our husbands as a priority under God, we will never feel that connection we so strongly desire.

IN REFLECTION

- Do you consider God the head of your household? Do you put your husband as the first priority after God?
- Have you ever put a list of your priorities on paper? I highly recommend spending some time honestly making that list.
- Do you want your husband to place your children as a higher priority than you?
- How can you expect a long-term covenant, when you are neglecting and dishonoring your husband in this area?
- If your children don't see this alignment and example in your home, are you willing to sabotage their futures by the choices you are making now? To put it in another way, aside from being the example: If you aren't willing to put your husband as the priority over your children, do you think they will benefit from an example of divorce or a loveless, disrespectful marriage?
- What changes can you make now to put your husband back at the top of the list, right after God?

Chapter 13

CHEERLEADER

Who is your husband's biggest cheerleader?? If the answer to that question isn't YOU, then you have a big problem.

When we first fell in love, our husbands could do no wrong. They were handsome and smart and funny and...perfect. We encouraged them and uplifted them and made them feel like a million bucks. That is probably one of the reasons he asked you to marry him in the first place. He felt great around you. He felt like he could conquer the world - he did, after all, capture the heart of his Princess.

When we fell in love, and when the blinders were on, we could see the hero and world conquerors in our husbands. We believed we would move forward in life and achieve whatever dreams we had. For some it was to start a family. Some maybe had the vision of the perfect house. Some thought of material things and for others it may have been emotional dreams or ideals of security. We believed our husbands could be CEO or business owners or the top of whatever craft they were in. We believed they were the best man for whatever the job was. We believed they could darn near walk on water.

I think the honeymoon phase of our relationships is really a gift from God. It is almost as though God shared with us a small glimpse of the man our husband was created to be. God knew we would go through struggles, but if we could think back and appreciate what we saw in our husbands back then, we could take that image and use it for good. And the amazing thing is that God only gave us a glimpse. It could have been a few months or a few years, but that tiny glimpse was just a small picture, an initial road map or puzzle piece to all that COULD be to come. It is really a matter of perspective. Some look back and think they lost that man. The wise woman is the one who can take that little figment and realize what greatness is possible.

At some point, something changed. What changed? Can you pinpoint when your blinders came off, or was it over a period of time? Did he become less attentive? Did he spend more time at work? Did he become critical? At what point did you lose sight of your Prince Charming?

I truly believe that our Prince Charming is still inside the man we fell in love with. I think life happened and we got discouraged. Perhaps his promotion fell through. Perhaps you had to work and come home to deal with the household responsibilities. Perhaps you don't think he held up his end of the bargain. At some point, you inevitably stopped cheering for your husband. You may have been hurt or tired or just plain fed up. Regardless of when and how it happened, it is important that you spend some time thinking about the man you fell in love with and married. It is important so you can help dig through his layers of life to help find him again.

The layers of life that cover our Prince Charming can be exhaustive. They have had disappointments in their careers and businesses. They have had disappointments in their marriage. They have been scarred or hurt in ways just like we have. They counted on us to be their biggest supporter. They counted on us to lift them up and encourage them. They counted on us to tell them how awesome they are and to encourage them to move forward. They counted on us to always keep them a priority. They counted on us to fill their sexual needs and allow them to feel like a man. We have let them down in so many ways. With every disappointment or roadblock in their life, they need to know that no matter what, we are behind them and still believe in them. At some point we stopped, and it only pointed out, too blatantly, that we had lost faith in our Prince Charming. I think often, because of that, they have lost faith in themselves too. So the man we once loved and adored got buried, not only by life, but by us not backing them up.

How often have you nagged about him not meeting your expectations or not providing something that you wanted? How often have you complained about not moving ahead or not getting enough attention from him? How often have you complained about his lack of help with the children or with the house? How often have you made it all too clear your disappointment in him??

I know that all of the things that happen in life are not our fault. Often poor decisions put our husbands in the situations they are in. However, we do need to take responsibility for our actions and interactions, for our support or lack thereof, for our failures as a wife, helpmeet, best friend and lover. We honestly have no control over them and whether they are willing to change, but we do have control over how we interact with them and whether or not we keep cheering them on.

I believe if a husband knows his wife is standing behind him and supporting him, it gives him great courage. I believe that if he knows his wife will not point out his mistakes or poor decisions, he will feel safe to own up to them and learn from them. I believe that if he knows he doesn't have to fight his wife, he will be more inclined to seek counsel from wise men. I believe if he knows his wife is behind him and believes in him, he will move mountains to make her dreams come true.

So when was the last time you encouraged your husband? When was the last time he made a poor decision that you didn't point it out? When was the last time you said, regardless of how this plays out, you are behind him and support him? When was the last time you thanked your husband for all that he has done? When was the last time you told your husband he is a stud? When was the last time you smiled when he walked in the door and when he asked why you were smiling you told him it was because you are so happy to see his handsome face? Seriously, when was the last time?

No matter what has happened in the past, today is a great day to correct your mistakes. You can't control him or what he does, but you can control your own interaction. You can reflect back on the vision of the man you married, that glimpse God gave you, and start complimenting and uplifting the man currently standing before you.

I do believe with all of my heart, that if you will get rid of all nagging and switch to uplifting and empowering, you will see miraculous improvement in your marriage. He doesn't need another person or obstacle to fight; he needs his Princess cheering him on!

IN REFLECTION

- Are you your husband's biggest cheerleader?
- Do you encourage him or discourage him?
- Do you believe in him? Did you when you got married? What changed?
- Do you nag your husband or point out his faults?
- Do you complain about expectations or dreams not being met?
- Do you want to see your husband succeed?
- Do you want his and your dreams to come true?
- Do you think they will come true if you are not his biggest cheerleader?
- What changes could you make right now to start cheering your husband on?

SONG OF SOLOMON 7:1-9

1 [a]How beautiful are your sandaled feet, O queenly maiden. Your rounded thighs are like jewels, the work of a skilled craftsman.

2 Your navel is perfectly formed like a goblet filled with mixed wine. Between your thighs lies a mound of wheat bordered with lilies.

3 Your breasts are like two fawns, twin fawns of a gazelle.

4 Your neck is as beautiful as an ivory tower. Your eyes are like the sparkling pools in Heshbon by the gate of Bath-rabbim. Your nose is as fine as the tower of Lebanon overlooking Damascus.

5 Your head is as majestic as Mount Carmel, and the sheen of your hair radiates royalty. The king is held captive by its tresses.

6 Oh, how beautiful you are! How pleasing, my love, how full of delights!

7 You are slender like a palm tree, and your breasts are like its clusters of fruit.

8 I said, "I will climb the palm tree and take hold of its fruit." May your breasts be like grape clusters, and the fragrance of your breath like apples.

9 May your kisses be as exciting as the best wine, flowing gently over lips and teeth.[b]

Chapter 14

STAYING A PRINCESS

Song of Solomon is a story of true love. It is a story of a shepherd and a Shulamite woman. Their love endured many obstacles and temptations. It is a perfect analogy of Jesus and the bride of Christ. It is a visual story that some would describe as erotic or sensual.

Now, before I get to the point, I have to tell you a quick story. As I am writing this chapter, my husband is working in our office and I am working out in our bohio by the pool. I find it more peaceful to work here than in the office. Alex is working on a major project and is very focused on that. We both have Skype so we can message each other from where we are working. I couldn't remember how to spell erotic, so I asked him through chat on Skype. In about 10.2 seconds, he had left his desk and was beside me asking, "Why do you ask?" with a big smile on his face. There is nothing like a potential interlude to distract our husbands from what they are currently focused on. It still amazes me to this day.

Now, back to my point. I find it interesting that we put so much energy focusing on the imperfections of our husbands that we forget to look in the mirror at ourselves. Our husbands have let us down in so many ways. That is inevitable. But let us focus right now on us.

Taking care of ourselves is important. This includes our physical appearance as well as other areas of our life. First, let us take a look at the physical.

Do you look like you did when you fell in love? Do you take care of yourself and present yourself in as pleasing of a manner as you did back then? Probably not, and that is okay. As we age, things just change, and that is life. There are, however, certain things that we can control. How do we dress? How is our hygiene? Have we put on some weight? These are all areas we can control. Why have you stopped putting energy into yourself to be pleasing to your husband? There really is no good excuse outside of serious medical issues.

I realize some of this falls under what was discussed in the chapter about sex. But, whether we like it or not, it is a very important subject, so consider this review.

Like it or not, your lack of presentation is a sign of disrespect to your husband. It does not promote uplifting, encouraging and empowering him. It does not send him out the door every day empowered to fight the good fight to make all of your dreams come true. A husband, in my opinion, fights much harder to make dreams come true if he knows he is coming home to a Princess.

Like it or not, in today's day and age, men are bombarded with advertising and life that promotes beauty. Since they are visual creatures, they are constantly surrounded by things that try to get their attention. Billboards, advertising, internet, the new secretary who takes care of herself, the coffee girl who serves him coffee in her cute coffee outfit, the waitresses, the colleagues – an endless amount of potential attractions in the world around us. Why, if you love him, would you not want to do all that it is in your power to keep his attention lured to you? In a perfect world, men would not notice such things. But in the imperfect world we live it, they are bombarded with it. It is a very sad reality, but we can either disagree with the reality, or we can be the cute cheerleaders cheering our man on, uplifting him and empowering him so he can't wait to get home. Here is another crucial area where we have to make a choice. I fought it for so long, thinking that if my husband loved me, he wouldn't notice these other things. If he was a good man, he would just tune them out. But I finally realized after reading many books, that men are attracted to beauty. God made them that way. Satan definitely perverted the beauty, but men are attracted to beauty nonetheless. And I have come to realize that even the most Godly, well-intentioned husbands who absolutely adore their wives and wouldn't consider straying, are still aware of the lures and have to fight to not be sucked in. I finally, after years of fighting it, decided that I would do everything in my power to help my husband want to come home.

PROVERBS 14:1

1 *A wise woman builds her home, but a foolish woman tears it down with her own hands.*

There was a time in our marriage that my husband couldn't count on me. I was not uplifting him or cheering him on. I was disappointed in him and did not show him respect. I took care of myself and looked good when I left the house for work, looking good for my boss. Then when I came home, I threw on sweatpants or something else unflattering and put my hair up in a ponytail. I gained weight after having children and blamed it on baby fat. I felt he should love me looking frumpy or not. I did nothing to encourage him and his self-confidence. I rebelled because I thought he should be different.

Then I realized that I could keep going the direction I was headed and end up divorced, or I could change my ways. I chose change and I chose life and I chose to be the wife my husband needed me to be. If you would ask him today, I know my husband would tell you that I am his biggest cheerleader. I uplift him and empower him and speak words of life into him. I take care of myself and always try to be appealing to him. Some may call this crazy, and that is okay, because I have an incredible marriage with an incredible man.

Taking care of ourselves is not just a physical thing. It is reflected in our attitudes, our hopes, and our joy. Are we pleasant to be around? How is our mood and our outlook? What is our conversation like? I think as much as we should consider our physical appearance, unless our hearts and attitudes are right, we can be rockin' hot on the outside, yet still be unattractive to our man. They may still appreciate it and make an attempt to take advantage of it, but not without cringing a bit.

Often times, we don't think about the things we are allowing into our heads, which inevitably affect our view on life, our view towards our husband, the way we interact, whether we are satisfied or dissatisfied…on and on. It is amazing what an impact television or Internet or the news or gossiping friends can have on our well-being. It has been several years since we got rid of cable. It may sound extreme, but we realized the impact of the garbage we were watching. So we don't have cable. We don't watch television unless we are traveling. I must, however, admit that I do download Grey's Anatomy throughout the season. Even watching something like that once a week has an impact on me. But I can tell you for the forty or so minutes I spend watching that each week, I spend about ten to twenty hours reading

Christian fiction, Christian non-fiction, the Bible and self-help books. I download sermons and seek out things that will not screw up my emotions or expectations of my husband or depress me about life issues. I have about a zillion things that I could be doing, especially now that I am in the middle of writing this book, but a priority every day is putting "good stuff" into my brain. It is intentional.

I am not saying you have to get rid of cable or read as much as me, but I would caution you that whatever is going into your brain, whether it is through TV or what you are reading or who you are hanging out with, it does have a significant impact on your attitude and how you are receiving life. Inevitably, it is affecting the way you interact with your husband as well as everyone else. You might want to consider the impact.

IN REFLECTIION

- Do you take the time to be appealing to your husband?
- Do you look as good when he comes home as you do when you leave the house to go shopping, to work or to church?
- Have you relaxed in your appearance since getting married? If so, in what ways? What are you doing differently now?
- Do you make excuses for these changes? Children? Job? Too busy? Etc.
- Do you want your husband to be distracted or seduced by other women? What are you doing to keep that from happening?
- Hypothetically, if something happened to your husband and you found yourself single again, would you present yourself differently? What would you change? I suggest making these changes now!
- What are you reading or watching every day that has an impact on your attitude and the way you interact with others?
- Would your husband consider you appealing, not only in your appearance, but also in your attitude and interaction with him?

Chapter 15

PRAYER

Life and marriage may often feel out of control. We seek and desire a blessed marriage, but life often tends to get in the way. The beauty of prayer is that it is available every second of every day. Regardless of the time of day, we can always count on an audience with our Father. Prayer is one weapon that is so necessary for our marriage.

> MATTHEW 18:19-20
>
> 19 *"I also tell you this: If two of you agree here on earth concerning anything you ask, my Father in heaven will do it for you.*
>
> 20 *For where two or three gather together as my followers,[h] I am there among them."*

The Bible encourages prayer and thanksgiving. Our Lord wants to be part of our life and our marriage. He wants us to seek Him out for wisdom and guidance. He wants us to count on Him and know He safely holds us in His hands. He wants to bless us in every possible way. But we need to seek Him out in order to receive those blessings.

The Bible tells us that when two or more people come to Him in prayer, in agreement, our prayers will be answered. When a husband and wife pray together, it encourages and reinforces unity in the marriage. By kneeling at His feet and humbling ourselves before Him, we open up a relationship with Him and our Prince Charming that no one can touch. Only He can provide that hedge of protection that is needed for our marriages. Only He can heal our broken hearts and help us to love our spouse beyond what we would be capable of accomplishing on our own. Only He can provide the strength to sustain a marriage and help us reach a level that we could never have dreamed of. Speaking from personal experience, the strongest weapon we have is our Father.

Prayer is also vitally important when it comes to misunderstandings and conflict. Any time there is conflict in our marriage or if my husband is coming under attack, I have learned to pray for him. If I am mad at him or hurt by him, I pray for him, as well as me. This isn't always easy. But you have to assume any conflict is coming from satan. Satan does not want you to have a great marriage. He does not want your marriage and your relationship to be blessed. Satan wants to see marriages destroyed, and the minute there is conflict, the evil one is all over that. He puts thoughts in your mind as well as your husband's. He puts doubt and wrong thoughts in your head. The only way to fight his evil is to pray. Pray together. Pray separately. If you have a prayer team, ask for their prayers. Anytime we have conflict, we have dear friends we can call on to pray for us. We don't even have to tell them details. It is just a quick call or email saying "Please pray for our spouse, our marriage and our family." It is as simple as that. Then we let God do the work.

Have you noticed your husband being irritable? Has he lashed out at you or been unloving? Our first response is to get hurt or angry.

Our first response needs to be prayer. It is amazing and miraculous how prayer can diffuse a situation. It is amazing how asking for a blanket of protection over our husbands can calm their spirit and allow God to work on their heart. I am in awe of the power of prayer.

Knowing men come under temptation is another reason to pray for them. How simple it is to ask for protection for our husbands so that they may be delivered from temptation. How God must smile in heaven knowing we are asking him to look out for our husbands. When was the last time you prayed for your husband? I suggest you make it a daily habit.

There is nothing wrong with asking God for blessings. He wants to bless us. He loves us dearly. He wants our marriages to flourish and our unity to grow stronger. He wants us to be examples to other married couples and encourage them in their marriages. The covenant of marriage is a most remarkable gift from God, and no one wants to see us prosper in our marriage more than Him.

IN REFLECTION

- Do you pray? Why or why not?
- Do you specifically pray for your spouse? For a hedge of protection around your marriage? For deliverance from temptation for both you and your spouse?
- Do you pray for healing when your husband hurts you?
- Do you pray for forgiveness when you hurt your husband?
- Do you pray for God to help you love your husband, just as God loves him?
- Do you realize that when there is conflict, satan takes advantage of it? Are you aware that your negative thoughts or actions are encouraged by satan?
- When you are angry or hurt, is your first thought to pray?
- Do you have a specific prayer list of the things you would like God to fix or heal in your marriage or your spouse? Make a list of your desires and take them before the Lord.
- Do you have a friend or friends you can call on to pray for you, your husband, your family and your marriage? It is time to make a list. Please know that I am only an email or phone call away and I will gladly pray for you (email: me@mistystanczyk.com).

Chapter 16

MENTORS

When it comes to your marriage, who are your mentors? Who do you know that has a successful and prosperous marriage? Who are you seeking out to help you have a better marriage?

PROVERBS 15:22

22 Plans go wrong for lack of advice; many advisers bring success.

PROVERBS 12:1

1 To learn, you must love discipline; it is stupid to hate correction.

PROVERBS 12:26

26 The godly give good advice to their friends;[a] the wicked lead them astray.

The Bible mentions many times the importance of wise counsel. Counsel is getting input and direction from people who have gone before you who have what you desire. Since you are reading this book, it is safe to assume you want a blessed and fulfilling marriage. Do you have someone you can talk to who has a marriage that you admire? Please don't tell me you have your marriage discussions with your twice-divorced girlfriend. Please don't tell me you call your mom when times are tough. It is vitally important that you find a couple (or preferably couples) who have a prosperous marriage, and turn to them when the going gets rough. Nothing positive can come out of counseling with someone who has not obtained a great marriage. I also believe it is incredibly unwise to go to your mom in venting any frustrations. Don't get me wrong - I love, adore, respect and cherish my mom. We have a very close relationship and I appreciate her so much, but I have seen too many women go to their parents and have it affect their relationship between their parents and their spouse. Times may be tough, but you can get through them, and when you do, you do not want your parents to have a swayed view of your husband! I feel it is both disrespectful to your husband and it lacks the soundness you can get from someone impartial. I can tell you that I have never complained or vented to my parents about the shortcomings or disagreements with my husband. When Alex and I got together, as I mentioned in the beginning of this book, my parents thought he was the antichrist. After our years together, my parents have grown to love and respect my husband. Had I ever gone to them with a problem we had, it could have skewed their views and damaged a relationship that has prospered. Let's face it, when we are upset, we tend to focus our problems on what our husband is doing wrong. In reality, we are often as much to blame. Why tarnish your parents' view of your amazing husband when the problems can be overcome and they are as much your responsibility as his? Again, I would strongly discourage it; many marriages end in part due to the butting in and judgment of the in-laws. Not a wise move.

If you are having marriage issues and your counselors/mentors are unable to help further, seek the wise counsel of professional Christians. I am amazed to see Christians gain counsel from someone who does not follow Christian principals. If you go to a counselor who recommends, based on your issues or personalities, that you shouldn't be married, run from them as fast as possible. The Bible is very clear about what constitutes the right for divorce. It says nothing about an unloving or selfish spouse. It says nothing about just falling out of love. It says nothing about not getting along. The Bible states that divorce is allowed in the event of adultery, period…and even that is debatable. So unless adultery or abuse (and I am not using that term loosely) are part of your marriage, any counselor who encourages or accepts divorce under other circumstances is not counseling according to Biblical principles and is not credible.

As much as we love some of our friends, be very careful about taking any counsel from them. If you truly seek to prosper in life, the people you counsel with will determine your success or failure. I can't stress that enough!!

With that being said, it is also important who you associate with. Who are your friends and co-workers? Who do you talk to during the day? The reason association is so important is because you become who you hang around. If your husband is hanging out with guys who complain and downgrade their wives, that behavior wears off on your husband. If you are hanging around ladies who gossip and complain, that will wear off on you. Although our intentions may be good, bad behaviors and habits of others will inevitably wear off on us. Are you hanging around friends who uplift and show respect to their husbands, or are you commiserating with them on how their husbands suck? Your association and your counsel have a significant impact on the life you lead, the prosperity or lack thereof in your marriage and whether you are moving forward in your walk with the Lord and contributing your gifts and talents to help others. Association and mentorship have a huge impact on where you are today.

IN REFLECTION

- Who are your mentors?
- Do you have someone with a prosperous marriage that you can call upon for advice or direction?
- Are the people you take counsel or advice from people who have the things and successes you want in life?
- Have you thought about the people you hang around and how their views and opinions affect you?
- I suggest making a list of the people you confide in or take advice from and determine if they are qualified to give their opinion. Do they have what you want, specifically in regard to marriage?

Chapter 17

SUPPORTING HIS VISION

This is another area that I struggled with for a very long time. What is your husband's vision? Do you know? Does he have one? What are his goals and hopes and dreams? This is something you should know and have ingrained into your heart. God created each of us for a purpose. Too often we go through life and get distracted by the noise around us. We lose sight of vision and dreams and goals.

For a long time, my hopes and dreams were not congruent with my husband's. We both had our own agendas and were pushing to accomplish them. There was no unity, and by default there was conflict. I can't pinpoint the day or even the year necessarily, but at some point in the last five years, I laid my hopes and dreams at the altar, and submitted them to the Lord. He knew my heart and hopes and desires. But He made it clear to me that until I got on board and supported my husband, my dreams would not come to fruition. At that point, my husband and I came to a mutual agreement on where we were headed. I am beyond clear as to what my husband's vision is. I am clear on his gifts and talents and hopes and dreams. I support his vision and everything that comes with it completely. By putting my hopes and dreams on the back burner, so to speak, the unity we have experienced is beyond comprehension. And I can tell you, without reservation, that by laying my agenda on the altar and coming into unity with my husband, my deepest desires are coming into fruition as a result.

Our men are created for greatness. They have each been blessed with unique gifts and talents that direct them on their path in life and walk with the Lord. My husband is an incredible visionary. He can look into the distant future and plan for things that most people do not take the time to see. He is an incredibly gifted public speaker, teacher, mentor and leader. He is an international businessman who prospers based on his integrity, character, courage, boldness and faith. He is an incredible husband and provider. He is an awesome and loving daddy. He is a hero to me, and I respect him and adore him more than I could possibly express in words. He continues to grow and learn and strive to be a better man. He is humble and wise.

The funny thing is that I could see all of these things in him when we fell in love. Then life happened and I lost sight of the incredible man I first saw in him. I started losing hope. I started nagging and pointing out his failures and shortcomings. I withdrew from him and put up walls for fear of being hurt…again. I started complaining to my friends and having pity parties. I did not show him respect nor did I uplift and empower him in any way. He withdrew and lost hope. He put up walls to deflect my criticisms and disappointments. He lost the motivation and courage to excel or move forward. We both lost hope and were ready to throw in the towel. I blamed him. He blamed me. It was a terribly destructive cycle we were in. Thank God for dear friends who interceded and directed us to counseling. Thank God for Penny, the incredibly gifted woman we counseled with who made us each take personal responsibility. Thank God for holding us together with a string, His string, until we were ready to take responsibility and make good choices to choose life and move forward. Thank God for the healing necessary to get over past hurts that ran so deep I thought they were impossible to get over. Thank God for loving us so much that since we didn't give up, He didn't either. I thank God every single day for keeping us together when the world and so-called friends encouraged us to go our separate ways. I can honestly say that with all of the garbage we went through, and there were mountains of it, I would do it all again if I had to, to get to where we are today.

Slowly but steadily I started to focus on that man I knew my husband could be. Slowly but steadily I worked on me, to become a better wife. I read books. I sought out counsel from people who had the marriages I so desired. I started complimenting my husband and focusing on the good. I stopped nagging and blaming and complaining. I learned to speak words of affirmation to my husband. I learned to submit to him and made a conscious choice to allow him to be the head of our household (next to God). I deferred to his decision when we could not come to an agreement. I supported him and backed him up in raising and disciplining our children. I went to God for healing when the hurts and memories came back to the surface. I prayed for our marriage and for my husband. I prayed that God would make me a good wife. I prayed that God would help me love my husband the way he does. I prayed that God would help me see my husband as the man he could be - the man God created him to be. I kept my hopes and dreams on the back burner and chose to follow my husband's lead. I cheered him on. I no longer pointed out when he made a bad decision. I gave him the freedom to make mistakes and let him know that I would stand behind him regardless of the outcome. It was a long road, and I was not perfect by any stretch of the imagination. I screwed up all of the time. But I honestly believe that God chose to bless us the more we chose to follow Him and do what was right. I honestly believe God created my husband for greatness. I honestly believe he needs my help to achieve that greatness. And I honestly want to see my husband be the man God intended him to be. I now feel that as his wife, that is part of my purpose and calling.

As I mentioned, I put my hopes and dreams on the back burner and chose to follow my husband. It took several years to get this right. But I sit here writing this today, in a hotel room in Addis Ababa, Ethiopia. For several years now I have felt called to get involved in work with orphans in Africa. Since I had laid my dreams at the altar, it meant waiting on the Lord for His timing. I supported my husband unconditionally and put my dreams aside. But today I sit here writing this, one of my dreams coming to fruition. By the grace of God and by my husband's obedience and hard work, I am realizing one of my dreams. I am here on my first mission trip, to serve orphans in several different orphanages. I am here to learn more about a project so near and dear to my heart: Acacia Village. I waited years to be able to embark on my vision, and I believe we have been blessed for our patience and persistence in following God's plan. My whole point of this is for you to know that by supporting my husband and his vision, I too have been blessed to realize mine. This is just one example of the results of following God's plan and supporting our amazing husband. My heartfelt plea to you would be to follow in my footsteps. My hope and desire is that you can uplift and empower your husband, support his vision, so he can become the man God intended him to be. As a result, you too will see your dreams come true.

Another dream of mine is to be able to fund Acacia Village in Ethiopia with the intent of taking the prototype of that project and expanding it throughout Africa and other countries. At the end of this book, there is information on this remarkable project. As one person, we can only do so much. But when a group of believers come together for a common good, I do believe with all of my heart that the Lord will bless the work. After discussing it with my husband, we have decided that 50% of any profits from this book will go directly to funding Acacia Village in Ethiopia, and hopefully beyond. I believe with the joint efforts of many, we can make great changes in this world. My vision doesn't have to be your vision. Each of us is called for a different purpose. But please know that by reading this book, not only are you moving towards a blessed marriage, you are also contributing to the lives of children around the world. What a blessing you are!

IN REFLECTION

- Do you know what your husband's vision is? Does he have one? Do you two discuss these sorts of things?
- Do you have your own vision and direction you are heading towards?
- Have you ever sat down and set goals with your husband? Have you ever talked about your dreams?
- Do you believe your husband was created for greatness? For a purpose? Do you feel you were created for a purpose? Do you realize that you were created for greatness as well?
- Do you have any idea of the blessings God wants to bestow on you and your marriage?
- Do you realize that if you are willing to learn and grow, God would love to use you in mighty ways? The same goes for your husband!
- Are you willing to support your husband's vision?
- Would you be willing to put your dreams and visions on the back burner and focus on helping your husband in unity?
- Do you realize that everything is in God's timing? Do you realize that every event in our life, whether good or bad, is God preparing us for our purpose? That without learning and growing through our struggles, we are delaying those dreams and visions?
- Have you ever sat down and made a list of your dreams

or goals? I would encourage you to take out a piece of paper and put 30 items down, either goals you want to accomplish, things you hope to acquire, or whatever you want to put on the list. Encourage your husband to do the same. Then compare your lists. Not only will you learn a lot about your husband, but hopefully you will find some unity that both you and your husband can focus on.

PROVERBS 12:4

4 A worthy wife is a crown for her husband, but a disgraceful woman is like cancer in his bones.

"I take you to be my wedded husband. To have and to hold, from this day forward, for better, for worse, for richer, for poorer, in sickness and in health, to love and to respect and to cherish, 'till death do us part. And hereto I pledge you my faithfulness."

Chapter 18

FOR BETTER OR FOR WORSE

When we enter into the covenant of marriage, we are full of hopes and dreams. We do love and we do respect and we do cherish. Our intentions are good, and we expect to live happily ever after.

Our hopes are to live "for better and for richer and in health," but life doesn't always work out that way. What happens when the "for worse or for poorer or in sickness" come along? Were you serious about your words before God? Because here is the sad reality in this fallen world...they (those hard times) will come...it is inevitable. But are you the woman of your words?

At some point after the honeymoon stage of our relationship, we start to see our husband's faults. We may experience financial issues or health issues. Our fairy tale isn't looking so fair any more. Now it is time to put action to what we professed before family and friends. When the "for worse, for poorer and in sickness" come along, it is then that we need to lean on our Lord and be the wife our husband needs us to be.

You may be saying by now that I am out of touch with reality, and what about the responsibility of our husbands. Well, this book is written by a woman, for women, with the hope that they could enjoy the blessed marriage I enjoy. So, regarding the men, this book isn't about them. If I can convince my husband to write a book like this for the men, I will do that. And I can assure you he will be as hard on them as I have been on you. But this book is about us seeking out the most awesome marriage to the incredible man in our lives. It is a book about choosing to make choices and do things that we may not want to do. It is about choosing to do the right thing, regardless of how we are feeling. It is about choosing to honor God by helping our husbands be the incredible men God intended them to be.

So, back to "for worse and poorer and in sickness". It is time to step up and put our money where our mouth is. During the "for worse and poorer and in sickness" is when our husbands need us the most. It is during this time that we can choose to help them or sabotage them. When two stand together in unity, no problem is insurmountable. When we are fighting the problems on our own, we are bound to end up disappointed and broken.

It is during these bad times that we often retreat into ourselves. Our men feel like failures, and we reinforce that by our actions. When they are feeling weak or scared or like failures, we are the one healthy saving grace they can reach out to, aside from our Heavenly Father. If they cannot count on us, they tend to reach out to whatever or whoever can help them. It is during this time that affairs are born or our spouses are lost. It is during this time that we have the opportunity to be there for them and be their helpmeet.

When men are feeling like failures, the last thing they need is for their wife to reinforce that. What they need is their best friend and cheerleader to walk with them through the shadows of the valley of death. It is at this point that they need to know that the one person who means the most to them on the entire planet will not retreat.

They need to know that you meant what you said.

There is no excuse that justifies us letting our husbands down during this crucial time. Whether you realize it or not, if they just had you to count on through the struggles, you would make them stronger and more courageous. With God's help and your support, our men can make it through the valleys and come out on the other side successfully. By walking through the shadow together, your marriage and you as individuals will be blessed.

Women always talk about their desired marriage, but when times get tough, many back down and give up. I am here to attest that until you are willing to tackle the "for worses and for poorers and in sicknesses," you will NEVER achieve the marriage you desire or the intimacy and connection that is the desire of your heart, as well as the amazing blessings that come along with it. Without putting in the time and sweat and tears, you will never achieve the results you so desperately desire. And without going through the tough times, in my opinion, you just don't deserve it. It takes work. It takes making choices that you don't necessarily want to make. It takes selflessness and commitment. It takes courage. But most of all it takes love. And I am not talking about "feeling" love; I am talking about agape (selfless "action") love.

You have to be willing to allow your husband to fail, and fail with dignity. You have to be willing to keep your mouth shut and support him through the failures. You have to be willing to submit to him and support his vision. If you are willing to do that, you hold the key to your husband's successes, not just in marriage but in every area of his life.

I can't beg you enough to be willing to walk with your husband through the dark times and offer him the respect and encouragement he so desperately needs. You are the only person in the world who can take that walk with him and offer him the success of being the man God intended him to be. His success is literally in your hands. And, quite frankly, if you are unwilling to take that walk, it is as much your fault as his for the failures. I do believe God is counting on you to keep your word and help His son be a man of greatness. I believe God will bless you beyond comprehension if you do.

IN REFLECTION

- When you got married, were you committed to marriage for life, and serious about the commitment you made to your husband, before God?
- Have the "for worse or for poorer or in sickness" come into your marriage?
- If you are the one person your husband needs, are you willing to let him down just because it is easier and less painful to give up? Do you think that would be honoring God?
- Do you believe that you will ever achieve the marriage you desire without working and committing through the struggles?
- If this was your child, would you give up as easily? Perhaps now would be a good time to reaffirm your vows.

Chapter 19

GOLDEN HOUR

Aside from everything else mentioned in this book, there is one specific additional thing that Alex and I have incorporated into our marriage and into our life. My husband adopted the term "Golden Hour" quite some time ago, so that is how we refer to it. In the mornings, when we wake, we make a conscious effort to start the day out on the right note. First we get our cup of coffee with cream, and then we head out to the bohio (Spanish word for hut-like a covered patio area) by the pool. We sit and thank God for all of our blessings and appreciate the new day He has laid before us. We both have our Bibles and generally at least one other book that we are reading individually. These other books have to do with some sort of growth, whether it be in our marriage, our walk with the Lord, leadership, business development or any kind of personal development. We sit in the quiet and read individually. When we read something that strikes us as significant, we share it and often some sort of discussion evolves from that. We also talk about our future, our vision, our hopes and our dreams. We start the day off with unity.

We recently returned from a month of travel, and by the time we got home, our unity was a little off. We sat down, talked about it and realized that over the last month, we had only exercised our "Golden Hour" a handful of times and division was beginning to creep in. We identified the problem and immediately addressed it by talking it out and re-clarifying our vision and direction. This has really been a vital part of keeping our marriage and friendship strong.

I know there are some of you who have conflict with such an exercise due to schedules or perhaps different beliefs. I understand that. However, I believe if there is a will, there is a way to make some sort of devoted quality time with your spouse. Perhaps you need to start out by setting aside devoted time just for you. Grab your Bible and a Christian marriage book or some other positive personal development book, and spend time growing every day. Spend time talking to God, sharing your hopes and your dreams and praying for your marriage and your spouse. If there are issues you are dealing with, share them with the Lord and ask Him for guidance and healing or whatever it is that you need. It all starts right there. Most importantly, ask God to show you the areas YOU need to work on. Remember, you can't change anyone other than yourself, and if you are like me, there are ALWAYS areas that need to be addressed.

One other comment about our "Golden Hour" is that our children know that during this time, they are not to interrupt us (unless in the case of an emergency, obviously). Our children respect our time, stay in the house and wait until we are done. They see it as an important part of our marriage, and I hope by example, it is something they will incorporate into their lives as they grow.

IN REFLECTION

- Do you and your spouse make a conscious effort to be together and communicate every day?
- Do you take time every day to spend time in prayer, thanksgiving, and some kind of personal development?
- What are your excuses if you are not doing this?
- What can you stop doing every day to make time for this? Less TV? Less computer? Less talking on the phone? Make a list of little things that you can cut out to make it happen. Another option would be to get up a little earlier. If you make this a habit, I am certain you will determine it to be very valuable.
- Are you willing to make time, regardless of the many excuses you could use?

Misty & Alex Stanczyk

Chapter 20

YOU ARE MY HERO

Alex Stanczyk, this chapter is dedicated to you. You are my hero! I still remember the day we met and how our relationship evolved from there. You intrigued me with your dreams and goals and your hope for the future. You gave me vision and a chance to hope and dream again. You supported my dreams and never once challenged them. You swept me off my feet, and I was never the same again.

Over the last 15 years, we have definitely seen "for better and for worse, for richer and for poorer, in sickness and in health." We went through a long time of darkness and pain and suffering. For so long I failed you as a wife. I failed to uplift you and empower you. I discouraged you rather than encouraged you. I lost sight of the incredible man I saw when we first met. I was unappreciative and confrontational. I struggled for control and disrespected you so often. I was not a friend you could count on but rather an emotionally driven crazy woman;) There were so many times we could have thrown in the towel and I thank God for His grace and mercy in keeping us together. I thank you for never giving up on me.

Although I have failed you so often, you have shown me grace that can only come from God. You have led by example. You have continually worked on improving yourself and growing. Your courage and bravery amaze me daily. I admire and respect you more than words can express. You are a mighty man of valor. Your integrity and character is unwavering. You are kind and generous to so many. You are an amazing leader and teacher. I am in awe of your public speaking gift. You strive for excellence on a daily basis and don't accept excuses or defeat. You speak words of life into me, our children and everyone you come into contact with. You do what is "hard and necessary versus what is fun and easy." You don't shortcut the labor, and you strive daily to be a better man. Your businesses flourish, and you are the incredible international business man that I always knew you could be.

What peace it gives me that you choose to counsel with great men and seek God's path for your life. You make great choices and learn from bad ones. You understand that in order to succeed, you must go through some failures. You persevere where most men would quit.

You are an incredible Daddy to our children. I watch our boys walk in your footsteps. They respect you and admire you. They trust you and your counsel. The fact that they are learning from you is so great to witness. Our daughter thinks you walk on water. You have treated her like a Princess and she blossoms because of your constant affirmation of your love. I will never forget when she asked if you would marry her;) What a blessing it would be for her to find a husband such as you.

You are an amazing husband. You are my best friend and I trust you completely. I trust your judgment and have no problem submitting to you, for I know you have my best interests at heart. You are unselfish and forgiving. You are patient with me and gracious when I am undeserving;) You have provided me with a lifestyle that I never dreamed possible. You continue to push me to grow and be all that God intends me to be. You support me and my dreams and accept them as your own. You are such a blessing in every area of my life, and I thank God for you every day.

Alex Stanczyk, you are a giant among men. I am so honored to be your wife!!

PSALM 118:1

1 Give thanks to the Lord, for he is good! His faithful love endures forever.

MATTHEW 7:7-8

7 "Keep on asking, and you will receive what you ask for. Keep on seeking,
and you will find. Keep on knocking, and the door will be opened to
you.
8 For everyone who asks, receives. Everyone who seeks, finds. And to
everyone who knocks, the door will be opened.

PSALM 37:3-4

3 Trust in the Lord and do good. Then you will live safely in the land and
prosper.
4 Take delight in the Lord, and he will give you your heart's desires.

1 THESSALONIANS 5:16-18

16 Always be joyful.
17 Never stop praying.
18 Be thankful in all circumstances, for this is God's will for you who
belong to Christ Jesus.

MARK 9:23

23 "What do you mean, 'If I can'?" Jesus asked. "Anything is possible if a
person believes."

Chapter 21

BLESSED BY CHOICE

Love is a choice. Love is a verb. Love is an action word. Love in the verb form is necessary to a successful marriage. Everything you do in your marriage is a choice. You can choose to love, or choose to withhold love because you are hurt. You can choose to speak words of affirmation into your husband and speak life, or you can choose to speak negatively and speak death. You can choose to submit to and respect your husband, or you can choose to challenge and compete with him. You can choose to allow your vulnerability to show, or you can choose to keep up your walls and keep stonewalling. You can choose to have a healthy love life with your husband, or you can choose to withhold that intimacy and create a further divide. You can choose to cheer him on, or you can choose to beat him down like the rest of the world. You can choose to take care of yourself and be appealing to your husband, or you can choose to encourage him to look elsewhere. You can choose to allow your husband to head the household and keep him the highest priority, or you can choose to allow others priority. You can choose to pray for your husband and your marriage, or you can choose to allow satan access. You can choose to mentor, counsel and associate with great people who want to see you succeed, or you can choose to associate with those who want to keep you at their level. You can choose to put your dreams and goals second and be unselfish to lift up your husband, or you can selfishly focus on your agenda. You can choose to stick it out through "worse, poorer and in sickness," or you can give up when the going gets tough and never reach your full potential. You can choose to forgive, or choose to hold grudges. You can choose to show love, or choose to hold it back. You can choose to be selfless, or choose to be selfish. You can choose to make the first move, or choose to wait for him. You can choose to work on you, or you can choose to try and change your husband. You can choose to go above and beyond what is called of you, or you can choose to just get by. You ultimately control the final outcome by the choices you make or fail to make.

My hope and prayer for anyone reading this book is that you would choose to dig your Prince Charming out from the stack of garbage that you have helped to bury him in. My hope and prayer is that you take seriously the significance you play in the successes and failures of not only your marriage but your husband's life endeavors as well. I promise if you are willing to pull out a shovel and start digging, with help from God, you will find that Prince Charming that you married. I believe with all of my heart that the man that you married is still there under the debris. He is still handsome and kind and a warrior and a winner. Whatever you fell in love with him for, I would encourage you to dig. The man you married and all of his wonderful and amazing and individual things that made him special - they are still there. He just needs your respect, support, encouragement, uplifting, patience and love to bring it back out.

It may take a month or it could take years. As a daughter of the King, you are equipped for the task. If you are willing to go through the pain and sacrifice to dig him out, I can promise you that you will look back and be willing to do it all over again to get to the place your marriage can be. Your marriage will be blessed if you will just stick it out. Your husband will be blessed because his secret weapon was willing to go to any length for him. I can tell you from experience, it is possible.

CHECK YOURSELF…

Show respect - unconditionally

Are you being disrespectful in any areas?

Speak life into your husband

Are you building him up by the words coming out of your mouth?

Are you telling him how awesome he is?

Submit and not compete

Are you allowing him to lead you and your family?

Allow him to fill your needs

Are you allowing him to rescue you in any way?

Hook him up

Please don't tell me you have a headache!

Excuses are not an option.

Keep him a priority

Next to God, he should be your top priority.

Support and cheer him on

Does he know you are standing with him?

Are you his biggest cheerleader?

Take care of yourself

Are you making an effort to be appealing to him?

Are you taking care of yourself?

Pray for him

This is vital! He needs your prayers!!

Seek wise counselors and association

Who are you mentoring with?

You become who you hang around.

Support his vision

Do you know his vision, and are you on board??

Stick with him in the tough times

Are there problems or situations you are dealing with?

Are you resolved to get through these issues?

I encourage you to do the following exercise and evaluate where you are. Please be honest with yourself.

Positive Qualities of my Prince Charming…why I fell in love with him:

1.
2.
3.
4.
5.
6.
7.
8.
9.
10.

Take a blank piece of paper if you need more room.

Negative Qualities of my Prince Charming

1.
2.
3.
4.
5.
6.
7.
8.
9.
10.

My Positive Qualities

1.
2.
3.
4.
5.
6.
7.
8.
9.
10.

My Negative Qualities

1.
2.
3.
4.
5.
6.
7.
8.
9.
10.

Grab a blank piece of paper if you need more room;)

With your ***husband's positive qualities***, meditate on them daily if not more.

With your ***husband's negative qualities***, pray for him and whatever they are.

With ***your positive qualities***, appreciate where your strengths are.

With ***your negative qualities***, this is really where you need to focus. You can't change your husband. You can pray for him and ask God to help you love him. But you can change yourself, and there are no doubt areas that YOU need to focus on. If you spend your time focusing on this list, you will be amazed at the results you will see.

Acacia Village

With over 40 million orphans in Africa, this orphan crisis is the epic problem of our time. Acacia Village Ethiopia www.acaciavillage.org helps address this emergency by providing forever families for thousands of children. This is an incredible opportunity to change and save lives for generations, by breaking the cycle of desperation.

Christian World Foundation (CWF) has negotiated a low cost lease with the Ethiopian government to build a campus to include a Children's Home, Children and Women's Health Clinic, Life Skills School and Christian Chapel. This campus will also include facilities for adoptive parents when they travel to complete their adoptions and housing for people who journey to Acacia Village for medical and church mission trips.

CWF is in the process of conducting a $3.7 million campaign to build Acacia Village. $725,000 has been raised so far. Construction of the Children's Home for 250 orphans is under way and we will build the remaining facilities as churches and individuals continue to fund our efforts.

Acacia Village will impact hundreds of adoptive families each year, but it will also help thousands of women and children in the surrounding area. Food distribution, medical care and vocational training will provide opportunity and hope for many.

CWF currently supports over 500 children in Ethiopia who will not be adopted. We provide food, clothing, education and an opportunity to play soccer. The number of children served in the local community will increase once Acacia Village is build.

The impact of Acacia Village is vast: sheltering orphans waiting to be adopted, help for families during the adoption process, immunizations and medical care for women and children in the community, a lighthouse of evangelism and a launching pad for many other ministries in Africa and throughout the world.

If you would like more information about being involved with building Acacia Village, contact Louis Fawcett, Director of Development at louis@cwa.org/.

ACACIA VILLAGE ETHIOPIA: PROGRAM OVERVIEW AND OUTLINE

BUILD ACACIA VILLAGE. BE ACACIA VILLAGE.

The background for this model of collaborative impact is simply that Christian World Foundation (CWF) recognizes that there are many parts of the Body of Christ, and that we will be most effective in impacting the world if we work together in a way that maximizes the opportunity for each "part" to fully express its gifts. In the case of CWF's Acacia Village project, God has provided us with an opportunity, a platform and strong relationships in Ethiopia that have the potential to impact the lives of many people in that country. But we realize that CWF cannot make that impact alone.

BUILD ACACIA VILLAGE

Building Acacia Village is really more than uniting bricks and mortar; it is the creation of a center for service to people in the name of Jesus.

Leveraging existing Christian World Adoption (CWA) infrastructure and experience in Ethiopia, building Acacia Village will impact the world in many important ways, including:

1. Acacia Village will shelter up to 500 orphans each year who are in transition from loneliness to permanent, loving families through the efforts of Christian World Adoption. Acacia Village will serve as a safe environment for these new relationships to begin.
2. Acacia Village will provide medical treatment and education, including English instruction and Bible training, for children.
3. Acacia Village will serve as a lighthouse in the community, reaching out to the local community to provide health related information and medical care for women. Women's health in Ethiopia is a key concern. Acacia Village will provide direct care for women while connecting them to a world of health resources through the internet.
4. Acacia Village will include accommodations for parents completing their adoptions, and also for mission teams intending to serve alongside CWF and/or CWA in Ethiopia.
5. Acacia Village will provide jobs for Ethiopian citizens.
6. Acacia Village witnesses to God's work to help people, one at a time.

Building Acacia Village is about financially providing resources for the construction and up-fitting of facilities in Ethiopia as well as the development and implementation of programs to be offered there.

BE ACACIA VILLAGE

Just as the acacia tree casts a vast shadow, providing shelter to many, CWF believes that those people whom God has impassioned with the vision for Acacia Village will allow its impact to spread through them; not only in Ethiopia, but here in the United States.

As families return from their adoption travel to Ethiopia, they re-enter their community with a child who will enrich the lives of many. When church and medical mission teams travel to Ethiopia their lives are changed, and those they influence hear and see the change – and the reason for it. The stories they tell about work in Ethiopia, and the new perspective on God's work they witnessed will lead others to be involved in this opportunity to save and change lives, perhaps for eternity. Acacia Village is in the faces of adopted children, in the hearts of adoptive parents, on the lips of those who tell others and in the hands of all who have a part in raising support for this ministry.

CWF intends to partner with those individuals, churches and businesses that it appears share a burden for making a difference in Ethiopia. We are currently in the process of further developing the programs to be offered at Acacia Village and, at the same time, developing relationships with people and organizations who may be prepared to be a part of delivering those services the people of Ethiopia.

Potential partnerships may include:

- Advocacy for adoption and involvement in encouraging adoptive families
- Providing educational resources and for the needs of staff (support, training)
- Providing medical equipment and professional resources
- Helping to develop awareness building tools, both in Ethiopia and the U.S.
- Providing financial resources to support the daily needs of children in transition
- An emphasis on women's health and education

Being Acacia Village is about pressing into relationships in order to see how we can accomplish together what we could not do apart. This may mean personal service, advocacy, equipping and/or financially resourcing those who may be involved on the front lines of service.

In so far as people in the US participate in accomplishing these goals, they are being Acacia Village. The branches of the Acacia Tree stretch far and wide. They involve many and serve many.

ACACIA VILLAGE PROGRAM DETAILS

The following is an outline of services provided and supported in each structure at Acacia Village:

CHILDREN'S HOME

This is a transitional home for 250 orphans at a time who are waiting to be adopted. The goal is for each child to be adopted within eight months. Facility will include:

- Dining Hall
- Kitchen
- Laundry Room
- Fenced Play Area
- Toddler Play Room
- Offices
- Three (3) floors of dormitory housing
- Nannies' apartments on each floor

LIFE SKILLS ENRICHMENT CENTER

Central to the vision for Acacia Village is that it would be a place of healing and transition while children wait to be placed with their forever families. The time they spend at Acacia Village won't be idle. Rather, we intend to seize the opportunity to prepare the children with life skills and education, including English lessons and Christian education.

The focus for the Life Skills School will be helping the children develop age-appropriate perspective on their transition into a family and to help equip them for their new life. For example, CWA will create audio-visual tools that will provide them with guidance and assistance in learning some of the language and also give them some understanding of what life in America may be like.

In partnership with the Women's and Children's Health Clinic, will provide:

- Physical fitness in the Gymnasium
- Vocational training for women and older children

- Computer and Internet training and usage
- Dance instruction
- Art instruction
- Music instruction
- Age appropriate classes in English, Math, Bible and Life Skills

WOMEN'S AND CHILDREN'S HEALTH CLINIC

This clinic will serve the children of Acacia Village as well as women and children in the surrounding community of Sabeta (15km West of Addis Ababa). The clinic will be a lighthouse for women to receive information about health and a place find empowerment through connections to the outside world. With computers available in Amharic (the official language of Ethiopia), women will have access to life changing health education.

Year round staff will provide infrastructure and support. Health services will be provided according to a posted schedule for the community. 1-2 week mission teams will rotate through Acacia Village providing additional services depending on the expertise of the team.

Local community needs will be evaluated on an ongoing basis and new programs initiated as the needs are presented.

Year Round Services for children to include:

- Immunizations
- Medical evaluation for adoption
- Treatment of minor illnesses and injuries
- Referral and transportation for major illnesses and injuries
- Age appropriate health, hygiene and nutritional education

Year Round Services for women to include:

- Prenatal education
- Prenatal vitamins
- Birth control education
- Immunizations
- Nutritional education
- HIV education
- Cooperation with the Addis Ababa Fistula Hospital
- Abortion hazard education
- Computers with internet (in Amharic) to connect women with global educational opportunities. Will include primer on using computers.

1-2 Week Clinics for Women and Children Performed by Mission Teams to include:

- Eye care
- Vocational skills training for older children and women geared toward local employment opportunities
- Ear, Nose and Throat evaluation and treatment
- Sonograms for pregnant women
- Breast cancer screening
- Orthopedics

FAMILY HOME

The Family Home will provide 15 suites to house families completing their adoptions and mission teams visiting for 1-2 weeks.

CWA ADMINISTRATION BUILDING

The CWA Administration Building will be the headquarters for CWA operations in Ethiopia and for all of Africa.

CHAPEL

The Chapel at Acacia Village will be open for regular services of Christian worship as well as personal devotional time.

GROUNDS

The grounds of Acacia Village will include basketball and volleyball courts, playground, green space and a garden (for joy and education). Acacia Trees will be planted in honor of President Girma.

www.acaciavillage.org
Build Acacia Village. Be Acacia Village.

Louis Fawcett
Director of Development
Christian World Foundation
4424 Erskine St.
Columbia, SC 29206
704-798-2795
www.ChristianWorldFoundation.org
www.cwa.org

Grrls4God.com

Grrls 4 God, or "G4G", is a membership based society of women for women. G4G is expected to go live in early 2010.

The G4G website is www.grrls4God.com

Misty describes G4G like this: "We are all screwed up in our own special way, regardless of where we come from. We all have issues from our past or things we are currently going through. Often times, we think there is no one who can relate...or if they can, the subject may be taboo. These issues can include divorce, abuse, infidelity, abortion, abandonment, addictions and loss, just to name a few. The list goes on and on. The goal with G4G is to find women who have dealt with these issues, have been through the healing and redemptive process, and are willing to take the hand of others going through the same struggles. It is a mentorship alliance of sorts. I believe part of our responsibility as Christians is to get rid of our pride and judgment, and be the hands and feet for Christ, to help others walk through the healing process."

Currently G4G is looking for women who are willing to contribute in the following areas:

- G4G Mentors - women who are willing to share their story and experiences to help mentor other women through the same struggles. Please email your stories and contact info to mentors@grrls4God.com.

- G4G Researchers and Writers – These brave ladies will research articles and books to help provide solid Biblically based information on the challenges we face, and suggestions on how to overcome them.
- G4G Moderators – Anyone who wishes to assist in making the G4G web-community a comfortable place to be. Moderators will monitor and participate in the discussions on the G4G community website and ensure that interaction among our members is pleasant and non-offensive.
- Women who are willing to share their personal stories of going through or overcoming challenges of life. Stories may be used in Misty's next book "*We're All Screwed Up In Our Own Special Way–taking life's experiences and helping others*". Before any story is used, we will obtain permission from the author. If you wish to remain anonymous, we would be happy to change the name in the book. Some stories may also lead to individual books in cooperation with the original author.

If you are interested in participating in any manner listed above or have thoughts on how you can contribute to the team, please email us at g4gteam@grrls4God.com.

As individuals, we can only do so much, but as a team of women who love God, we can come together and make a huge impact. We would love to have you part of the team!!

Earn Additional Income

One issue that tends to affect marriages is finances. In the early days of our marriage, finances certainly impacted our lives and contributed to many struggles. One major lesson we learned is that having multiple streams of income helps to build a "financial house" that is not easily blown over by economic storms.

Especially in the US, there is a significant problem with savings. Many families may appear to be doing well, but debt is often times a problem. No matter how much money we make, debt can bring our houses crumbling down.

Since many non-profit organizations count on funding from people, we have created an additional income stream to help contribute to projects and causes near and dear to our hearts.

We are happy to offer you an opportunity to save in "tangible assets" as well as create an additional income stream for families wishing to do so.

The business is based around savings programs in pure gold and silver, minted and shipped from one of the most reputable Swiss refineries in the world.

You can either participate as a buyer of gold and silver, or you can choose to generate an income as well.

Regardless of which way you get involved, you will be contributing to projects including, but not limited to:

- Acacia Village in Ethiopia
- Funding orphanages and education in different countries around the world
- Building of the G4G Redemption Ranch which will minister to women and families without charge

For more information, please visit www.grrls4God.com/opportunity. You can also call 701-212-1165 or email: g4gtrust@grrls4God.com.

Working together we can make a difference.

Recommended Reading

Books addressing marriage and understanding our guys

Hung by the Tongue by Francis P. Martin (FPM Publications 1976)

Love & Respect: The Love She Most Desires; The Respect He Desperately Needs by Dr. Emerson Eggerichs (Thomas Nelson, Inc. 2004)

The Love Dare by Stephen and Alex Kendrick (B&H Publishing Group 2008)

The Five Love Languages by Gary Chapman (Northfield Publishing 1995)

Your Personality Tree by Florence Littauer (Thomas Nelson 1989)

7 things he'll never tell you... by Dr. Kevin Leman (Tyndale House Publishers, Inc. 2007)

What's He Really Thinking? by Paula Rinehart (Tomas Nelson 2009)

What a Husband Needs From His Wife by Melanie Chitwood (Harvest House Publishers 2006)

For Women Only by Shaunti Feldhahn (Multnomah Publishers, Inc. 2004)

The Lights of Tenth Street by Shaunti Feldhahn (Multnomah Publishers, Inc. 2003 – This is a wonderful fiction novel that reveals man's struggle with sexual lures and helps understand their perspective of that struggle.)